St. George Jackson Mivart

Modern Catholics and scientific freedom

St. George Jackson Mivart

Modern Catholics and scientific freedom

ISBN/EAN: 9783337282394

Printed in Europe, USA, Canada, Australia, Japan

Cover: Foto ©Lupo / pixelio.de

More available books at **www.hansebooks.com**

THE NINETEENTH CENTURY.

A MONTHLY REVIEW

EDITED BY JAMES KNOWLES.

No. 101, JULY 1885.

		PAGE
I.	The Khedivate of Egypt. By EDWARD DICEY	1
II.	The Work of Victor Hugo. By ALGERNON CHARLES SWINBURNE	14
III.	Modern Catholics and Scientific Freedom. By ST. GEORGE MIVART	30
IV.	A Swain of Arcady. By the Rev. Dr. JESSOPP	48
V.	Parliamentary Manners. By HENRY W. LUCY	58
VI.	Public Business in the House of Commons. By HENRY H. FOWLER, M.P.	69
VII.	Drink: a Last Word to Lord Bramwell. By the Ven. ARCHDEACON FARRAR	78
VIII.	To Within a Mile of Khartoum. By Capt. R. F. T. GASCOIGNE	88
IX.	Recent Progress in Biology. By Professor RAY LANKESTER	101
X.	The Armed Strength of Turkey. By WOODS PASHA	111
XI.	Mine Inspection: a Reply. By GEORGE BLAKE WALKER	124
XII.	Transylvanian Superstitions. By Mme. EMILY DE LASZOWSKA GERARD	130
XIII.	The True 'Scientific Frontier' of India. By JOHN SLAGG, M.P.	151
XIV.	England or the Admiralty? By H. O. ARNOLD-FORSTER	160

KEGAN PAUL, TRENCH & CO., LONDON.

PARIS: LIBRAIRIE GALIGNANI, 224 RUE DE RIVOLI.
AGENTS FOR AMERICA: THE INTERNATIONAL NEWS COMPANY, NEW YORK.

1885.

Price Half-a-Crown.   *All rights reserved.*

TWENTY ONE PRIZE MEDALS AWARDED.

Fry's Cocoa Extract

GUARANTEED PURE.

'There is no nicer or more wholesome preparation of Cocoa.'—*Dr. Hassall.*

ROWLANDS' ODONTO

Is the purest and most fragrant dentifrice ever made; it whitens the teeth, prevents decay, and gives a pleasing fragrance to the breath. All dentists will allow that neither washes nor paste can possibly be as efficacious for polishing the teeth and keeping them sound and white as a pure and non-gritty tooth powder; such Rowland's Odonto has always proved itself to be.

ROWLANDS' MACASSAR OIL

Has been known for the last 85 years as the best and safest preserver and beautifier of the Hair; it contains no lead or mineral ingredients, and is especially adapted for the Hair of Children. It can now also be had in a golden colour, as well as in the ordinary tint. Sold in usual four sizes. Ask any Chemist, Perfumer, or Hairdresser for Rowlands' articles.

The Nineteenth Century Advertiser, July 1885.

☞ *Advertisements should be sent to Hart's Advertising Offices, 33 Southampton Street, Strand, W.C. Bills for insertion should be delivered to the Printers, Messrs. Spottiswoode & Co., New-Street Square, by the 25th of the month.*

SAMPSON LOW, MARSTON, & CO.'S NEW BOOKS.

AN ENTIRELY NEW WORK. 'Now ready, at all Libraries and Booksellers,'
LORD SALISBURY.
THE LIFE AND SPEECHES OF THE MARQUIS OF SALISBURY, K.G. By F. S. PULLING, M.A., Exeter College, Oxford, sometime Professor of Modern History at the Yorkshire College, Leeds. 2 vols. with Photogravure Portrait, price 21s.

Now ready.
LIFE AND REMINISCENCES OF GUSTAVE DORÉ. Compiled from Material supplied by Doré's Relations and Friends and from Personal Recollections. With many Original Unpublished Sketches, and Selections from Doré's best Published Illustrations. By BLANCHE ROOSEVELT. 1 vol. large 8vo. cloth extra, price 24s.

New and Cheaper Edition of MR. FRANCIS GEORGE HEATH'S POPULAR WORK,
THE FERN WORLD. Illustrated with all the Original Coloured Plates and Woodcuts. Small 8vo. cloth, 6s.

Now ready, price One Shilling.
HARPER'S MAGAZINE, FOR JULY. Containing Frontispiece, 'PANDORA,' from the Painting by F. S. CHURCH, 16 ARTICLES, and 57 WOODCUT ILLUSTRATIONS. **HARPER'S YOUNG PEOPLE** for JULY, Illustrated, 6d.

THOMPSON HALL. By ANTHONY TROLLOPE. Illustrated. Price One Shilling. | **TIGERS AT LARGE:** Tales and Sketches. By PHIL ROBINSON. Price One Shilling.

BOOKS FOR SUMMER READING.

LOW'S STANDARD NOVELS.
Small post 8vo. cloth extra, price **6s.** each (except where otherwise stated).

By R. D. Blackmore.
Lorna Doone. (Also an Illustrated Edition, 31s. 6d. and 35s.)
Alice Lorraine.
Cradock Nowell.
Cripps, the Carrier.
Clara Vaughan.
Erema; or, My Father's Sin.
Mary Anerley.
Christowell : a Dartmoor Tale.
Tommy Upmore.

By William Black.
Three Feathers.
A Daughter of Heth.
Kilmeny.
In Silk Attire.
Lady Silverdale's Sweetheart.
Sunrise.

By Thomas Hardy.
A Pair of Blue Eyes.
The Return of the Native.
The Trumpet Major.
Far from the Madding Crowd.
The Hand of Ethelberta.
A Laodicean.
Two on a Tower.

By Joseph Hatton.
Three Recruits, and the Girls they left Behind Them.

By George Mac Donald.
Mary Marston.
Guild Court.
The Vicar's Daughter.
Adela Cathcart.
Stephen Archer, and other Tales.
Orts.
Weighed and Wanting.

By W. Clark Russell.
Jack's Courtship.
Wreck of the Grosvenor.
John Holdsworth (Chief Mate).
A Sailor's Sweetheart.
The Lady Maud.
A Sea Queen.
Little Loo.
My Watch Below.

By Mrs. J. H. Riddell.
Daisies and Buttercups: a Novel of the Upper Thames.
The Senior Partner.
Alaric Spenceley.
A Struggle for Fame.

By Victor Hugo.
Ninety-three.
The History of a Crime: the Story of the Coup d'État.

By Mrs. Cashel Hoey.
A Golden Sorrow.
Out of Court.

By Constance Fenimore Woolson.
Anne: a Novel. Third Edition.
For the Major. Illustrated, uniform with the above, 5s.

By Helen Mathers, Authoress of 'Comin' thro' the Rye,' 'Cherry Ripe,' &c.
My Lady Greensleeves.

By Mrs. Beecher Stowe.
Poganuc People: their Loves and Lives.
My Wife and I.
Old Town Folk.

By Lewis Wallace.
Ben Hur: a Tale of the Christ.

By Mrs. Macquoid.
Elinor Dryden.
Diane.

By Miss Coleridge.
An English Squire.

By the Rev. E. Gilliat, M.A.
A Story of the Dragonades.

By the Author of 'One Only,' 'Constantia,' &c.
A French Heiress in her Own Château. 6 Illustrations.

London : SAMPSON LOW, MARSTON, SEARLE, & RIVINGTON, Crown Buildings, 188 Fleet Street, E.C.

a

MESSRS. MACMILLAN & CO.'S NEW BOOKS.

By F. MARION CRAWFORD,
Author of 'Mr. Isaacs,' 'Dr. Claudius,' 'A Roman Singer,' &c.

ZOROASTER.

Two Volumes. Globe 8vo. 12s.

'Mr. Marion Crawford's new work is an agreeable excursion into the realms of historic romance, and exhibits at their best those qualities which distinguish him from other living American novelists—we mean his imagination and direct vigour...... *Zoroaster* will undoubtedly add to the author's repute.'—THE ATHENÆUM.

By HENRY JAMES.
STORIES REVIVED IN THREE VOLUMES. By HENRY JAMES, Author of 'The American,' 'The Europeans,' &c. 3 vols. crown 8vo. 31s. 6d.
*** The majority of the Stories contained in these volumes have not been previously published in England.

By CHARLOTTE M. YONGE.
THE TWO SIDES OF THE SHIELD. By CHARLOTTE M. YONGE, Author of 'The Heir of Redclyffe,' &c. 2 vols. Crown 8vo. 12s.

NEW BOOK BY SIR JAMES FITZJAMES STEPHEN.
THE STORY OF NUNCOMAR AND THE IMPEACHMENT OF SIR ELIJAH IMPEY. By Sir JAMES FITZJAMES STEPHEN, K.C.S.I., D.C.L., a Judge of the High Court of Justice, Queen's Bench Division. 2 vols. Crown 8vo. 15s.

NEW WORK BY MR. MATTHEW ARNOLD.
DISCOURSES IN AMERICA. By MATTHEW ARNOLD, D.C.L., LL.D. Crown 8vo. 4s. 6d. [*Macmillan's* 4s. 6d. *Series.—New Volume.*

POEMS. By MATTHEW ARNOLD. New Edition in Three Volumes. With additional Poems. Vol. I. Early Poems, Narrative Poems, and Sonnets. Vol. II. Lyric and Elegiac Poems. Vol. III. Dramatic and Later Poems. Crown 8vo. 7s. 6d. each.

BY R. CHENEVIX TRENCH, D.D.
POEMS. By R. CHENEVIX TRENCH, D.D. New Collected Edition, 2 vols. Extra fcp. 8vo. 10s.

MALTHUS AND HIS WORK. By JAMES BONAR, M.A., Balliol College, Oxford. Demy 8vo. 12s. 6d.

ON LIGHT. Being the Burnett Lectures. By GEORGE GABRIEL STOKES, M.A., F.R.S., &c. Fellow of Pembroke College, and Lucasian Professor of Mathematics in the University, Cambridge. First Course: *On the Nature of Light.* Second Course: *On Light as a Means of Investigation.* Crown 8vo. 2s. 6d. each.

NEW BOOK BY EDWIN A. ABBOTT, D.D.
FRANCIS BACON: an Account of His Life and Works. By EDWIN A. ABBOTT, D.D., Author of 'Bacon and Essex,' Editor of Bacon's 'Essays'; formerly Fellow of St. John's Coll., Camb. 8vo. 14s.
'Dr. Abbott has not merely studied deeply all Bacon's published writings, but has also shown great keenness of insight into the character that is revealed in them. Especially he has worked out the results of Bacon's hopefulness and self-satisfaction in a way which has never been attempted before.'—Professor S. R. GARDINER, in the *Academy*.

CARLYLE, PERSONALLY AND IN HIS WRITINGS. Two Lectures. By DAVID MASSON, M.A., LL.D. Extra fcp. 8vo. 2s. 6d.
'These lectures should be read by all admirers of Carlyle.'—SATURDAY REVIEW.

POPULAR EDITION, ONE SHILLING.
ANYHOW STORIES FOR CHILDREN. By Mrs. W. K. CLIFFORD. With Illustrations by Dorothy Tennant. New Edition. Crown 8vo. paper cover, 1s.; cloth, 1s. 6d.

GREEK TESTAMENT FOR SCHOOLS.
THE NEW TESTAMENT IN THE ORIGINAL GREEK. The Text Revised. by BROOKE FOSS WESTCOTT, D.D., and FENTON JOHN ANTHONY HORT, D.D. 12mo. cloth, 4s. 6d.; 18mo. roan, red edges, 5s. 6d.

EUROPEAN BUTTERFLIES. By FRANCIS DE V. KANE. With Copperplate Illustrations. Crown 8vo. [*Just ready.*

SECOND EDITION (FIFTH THOUSAND), REVISED AND ENLARGED.
TEXT-BOOK OF GEOLOGY. By ARCHIBALD GEIKIE, LL.D., F.R.S., Director-General of the Geological Survey of Great Britain and Ireland, and Director of the Museum of Practical Geology, London, &c. With Illustrations. Second Edition, Revised and Enlarged. Medium 8vo. 28s.

AN ATLAS OF PRACTICAL ELEMENTARY BIOLOGY. By G. B. HOWES, Demonstrator of Biology, Normal School of Science and Royal School of Mines, Lecturer in Comparative Anatomy, St. George's Hospital Medical School, London. With a Preface by Professor HUXLEY, F.R.S. Medium 4to. 11s.

MR. HENRY IRVING on THE ART OF ACTING.
See **The English Illustrated Magazine**
For JULY. Profusely Illustrated, price Sixpence; by post, 8d.

MACMILLAN & CO., London.

SMITH, ELDER, & CO.'S NEW BOOKS.

'One of the most entertaining books of the year.'—THE STANDARD.

NOTICE.—The THIRD EDITION of the 'LIFE OF FRANK BUCKLAND,' by his Brother-in-Law, George C. Bompas, is now ready. With a Portrait, large crown 8vo. 12s. 6d.

Now ready, price 12s. 6d. in cloth; or in half-morocco, marbled edges, 18s.
Vol. III. (Baker-Beadon) Royal 8vo., of

THE DICTIONARY OF NATIONAL BIOGRAPHY.
Edited by LESLIE STEPHEN.

*** *VOLUME IV. WILL BE PUBLISHED ON OCTOBER 1, AND THE SUBSEQUENT VOLUMES AT INTERVALS OF THREE MONTHS.*

FROM 'THE ATHENÆUM.'

'Perhaps the most satisfactory among the many satisfactory features in the second instalment of Mr. Leslie Stephen's great work is the comparatively short period of time which separates it from its predecessor.... There are no traces of undue hurry about this volume, which is in every respect equal to that which opened the series. The staff of contributors is strengthened by the addition of some well-known names. A few unimportant shortcomings in the matter of proportion and arrangement were discernible in the first part; in the present one there is hardly room for criticism on this score.... On the whole, there is little to criticise and much to admire in this volume, which, as we are glad to think, sees Mr. Stephen and his coadjutors fairly afloat on their great venture.'

FROM 'THE SPECTATOR.'

'Neither in fulness, in accuracy, nor in interest does the second volume show any falling off from its predecessor.... We heartily thank the editor and his contributors for this second instalment of a work the value and interest of which it is impossible to overrate, and which, we believe, will be hereafter considered as one of the most useful which the nineteenth century has produced.'

Now ready, 8vo. 12s. 6d. Volume III. of a New Translation in 4 Vols. of 'Don Quixote.'

THE INGENIOUS GENTLEMAN, DON QUIXOTE OF LA MANCHA.
By MIGUEL DE CERVANTES SAAVEDRA.

A Translation, with Introduction and Notes by JOHN ORMSBY, Translator of 'The Poem of the Cid.'
*** *Volume IV. completing the work will be published next Month.*

FROM THE 'PALL MALL GAZETTE.'

'Of Mr. Ormsby's version we may say that, judging from the two volumes already before us, it excels all previous versions in a certain union of accuracy and sobriety...... His book as a book is a very handsome one without being unwieldy. It has an excellent Introduction, bibliographical, biographical, and critical. His notes are excellent, short, to the point, and present at every occasion where the reader can justly demand them.'

NEW VOLUME of the 'STANDARD EDITION' of the COMPLETE WORKS of W. M. THACKERAY.

ROUNDABOUT PAPERS: the SECOND FUNERAL of NAPOLEON.
With 11 Full-page Illustrations and 54 Wood Engravings by the Author, CHARLES KEENE, and M. FITZGERALD. Large 8vo. 10s. 6d.

NEW VOLUMES OF SMITH, ELDER, & CO.'S POPULAR 2s. 6D. SERIES.

CARITA. By Mrs. OLIPHANT, Author of 'The Chronicles of Carlingford,' &c. Fcp. 8vo. limp cloth, 2s. 6d.

WITHIN THE PRECINCTS. By Mrs. OLIPHANT, Author of 'Carita' &c. Fcp. 8vo. limp cloth, 2s. 6d.

NEW VOLUMES OF SMITH, ELDER, & CO.'S POPULAR 2s. SERIES.

ROSSMOYNE. By the Author of 'Molly Bawn.' Fcp. 8vo. boards. Pictorial Cover, 2s.

DORIS. By the Author of 'Molly Bawn,' 'Mrs. Geoffrey,' &c. Fcp. 8vo. boards. Pictorial Cover, 2s.

MEHALAH: a Tale of the Salt Marshes. By the Author of 'John Herring' &c. Fcp. 8vo. boards. Pictorial Cover, 2s.

JOHN HERRING. By the Author of 'Mehalah' &c. Fcp. 8vo. boards. Pictorial Cover, 2s. [*In the press.*

*** *The following volumes of the 2s. Series can now be had in fcp. 8vo. limp cloth, price 2s. 6d. each:*—
MOLLY BAWN, PHYLLIS, MRS. GEOFFREY, AIRY FAIRY LILIAN, ROSSMOYNE, DORIS.

Just published. Demy 8vo. 14s. Vol. I. of

VON ZIEMSSEN'S HANDBOOK OF GENERAL THERAPEUTICS.

CONTENTS:—General Introduction by Dr. ZIEMSSEN. On the Dietary of the Sick and Dietetic Methods of Treatment by Professor J. BAUER. On the Kournies Cure by Dr. STANGE. Translated by EDWARD F. WILLOUGHBY, M.D.

*** *The Handbook will comprise 7 volumes, demy 8vo. with Illustrations, to be published at short Intervals. Volume II. will be ready on the 6th of July.*

London: SMITH, ELDER, & CO., 15 Waterloo Place.

KEGAN PAUL, TRENCH, & CO.'S LIST.

'A story which combines imagination, observation, and finish in a high degree.'
— ATHENÆUM.

NOTICE.—*The Third Edition of 'COLONEL ENDERBY'S WIFE,' a Novel by LUCAS MALET, is ready this day at all Libraries, in 3 vols.*

Just ready, crown 8vo. cloth, 5s.
SUAKIN, 1885.
BEING A SKETCH OF THE CAMPAIGN OF THIS YEAR.
BY AN OFFICER WHO WAS THERE.

The work contains the remarks of an eye-witness, and all the statistics and figures are taken from Reports, &c. sent to Lord Hartington, by the Officer Commanding the Troops at Suakin.

Elzevir 8vo. choicely printed on hand paper, cloth extra, gilt top, 6s.
SCEPSIS SCIENTIFICA;
Or, Confest Ignorance, the Way to Science; in an Essay of the Vanity of Dogmatising and Confident Opinion.
By JOSEPH GLANVILL, M.A.
Edited, with an Introductory Essay, by JOHN OWEN.

Crown 8vo. cloth, 7s. 6d.
THE CHURCH OF ENGLAND, AND OTHER RELIGIOUS COMMUNIONS.
A Course of Lectures delivered at the Parish Church of Clapham.
By ROBERT HOWARD, M.A.

Eighth and Cheaper Edition, crown 8vo. cloth, 1s. 6d.; paper covers, 1s.
FREE TRADE IN LAND.
By JOSEPH KAY.
Edited by his Widow.
With Preface by the Right Hon. JOHN BRIGHT, M.P.
And a review of recent changes in the Land Laws of England, by the Right Hon. G. OSBORNE MORGAN, Q.C., M.P.

Seventh Edition, small crown 8vo. cloth, 5s.
THE DISCIPLES.
By HARRIET ELEANOR HAMILTON KING, Author of 'Aspromonte,' 'A Book of Dreams,' &c.

Crown 8vo. cloth, 7s. 6d.
ONNALINDA: A ROMANCE.
By J. H. McNAUGHTON.

'I have read "Onnalinda" with attention and pleasure, and without stopping till I had finished it.'—The Right Hon. the EARL OF LYTTON.

'There is life and beauty in it, which I have much enjoyed.'—The Right Hon. JOHN BRIGHT, M.P.

Small crown 8vo. cloth, 3s. 6d.
LOUISE DE LA VALLIÈRE, AND OTHER POEMS.
By KATHERINE TYNAN.

'Very seldom is it our good fortune to close a volume of poems with such an almost unalloyed sense of pleasure, and, we may add, gratitude to the author...... Miss Tynan has a singular gift of music which makes her poems delightful to the ear, joined to an appreciation of nature and a thoughtful depth of sympathy which must appeal as certainly to the heart...... A book to own and treasure.'—GRAPHIC.

Just published, 1s.
THE FIGHTING OF THE FUTURE.
By Captain IAN HAMILTON, A.D.C.

London: 1 PATERNOSTER SQUARE.

GORDON'S JOURNALS
AT
KARTOUM.

NOTICE.—*This day at all Booksellers' and Libraries,* 'THE JOURNALS OF MAJOR-GENERAL C. G. GORDON, C.B., AT KARTOUM, *printed from the original MSS.,*' 650 *pp. demy 8vo. cloth, price* 21s.

Various Appendices, containing important Documents hitherto unpublished, and Letters from the MAHDI, SLATIN BEY, ABDEL KADER, *&c., as well as an Introduction and Notes by the Editor,* Mr. A. EGMONT HAKE, *Portrait, Maps, and Thirty Illustrations after Sketches by* GENERAL GORDON, *are included in the volume.*

London: KEGAN PAUL, TRENCH, & CO.

MR. T. FISHER UNWIN'S LIST.

LITERARY LANDMARKS of LONDON. By LAURENCE HUTTON. Crown 8vo. 7s. 6d. (post free).

'Mr. Laurence Hutton has worked out a felicitous idea with industry, skill, and success.'—STANDARD.
'Abounds with interesting facts.'—DAILY NEWS.

NEW NOVELS.

CAMILLA'S GIRLHOOD. By LINDA VILLARI, Author of 'On Tuscan Hills and Venetian Waters,' 'In Change Unchanged,' &c. 2 vols. crown 8vo. 21s. [*In the press.*

A NOBLE KINSMAN: a Novel. By ANTON GIULIO BARRILI, Author of 'The Devil's Portrait,' &c. Translated from the Italian by H. A. MARTIN. 2 vols. crown 8vo. 21s.

'The story of the loves of Renato and Margherita Altavillo is pure and charming, and there runs throughout it a strong current of dramatic incident.'—MORNING POST.

WILBOURNE HALL. By Mrs. CAUMONT, Author of 'Uncle Anthony's Note Book.' 2 vols. crown 8vo. 21s.

'There are some natural touches in "Wilbourne Hall." ...... May be read with considerable pleasure.'—ACADEMY.

CENTRAL ASIAN QUESTIONS: Essays on Afghanistan, China, and Central Asia. By DEMETRIUS C. BOULGER, Author of 'The History of China,' 'England and Russia in Central Asia,' &c. With Portrait and 3 Maps. Demy 8vo. 18s.

'Whether the views set forth are accepted or not, all must acknowledge the eloquence of the author, and the mass of information which he has brought together on the most burning question of the time in foreign politics.'—DAILY CHRONICLE.

THE MAHDI, Past and Present. By Prof. J. DARMESTETER. Illustrated. Sewed, 1s.; cloth, 1s. 6d. (post free).

'Pleasant and instructive reading.'—ATHENÆUM.

'EXPOSITIONS.' By Rev. SAMUEL COX, D.D., Author of 'Salvator Mundi' &c. Dedicated to Baron Tennyson. Demy 8vo. 7s. 6d. (post free).

'Independent thought, vigorous expression, and, what is better still, much heart-searching truth.'—LEEDS MERCURY.

THE UNKNOWN GOD, and other Sermons. Preached in St. Peter's, Vere Street, by Rev. ALEX. H. CRAUFURD, M.A., Author of 'Seeking for Light.' Crown 8vo. 6s. (post free).

'A volume of animated and interesting sermons.'—ACADEMY.

London: T. FISHER UNWIN, 26 Paternoster Square, E.C.

Now Ready, Vol. I. Demy 8vo. pages 538, price 20s.

A HISTORY OF PRIVATE BILL LEGISLATION.

By FREDERICK CLIFFORD, Barrister-at-Law.

EXTRACT FROM AUTHOR'S PREFACE.—In bulk and number local and personal enactments far exceed those of a public nature. For example, between 1800 and 1884, the number of Public Acts was 9,556, of Private Acts 18,497. No connected account of this great mass of private legislation has yet been attempted, though it has had momentous results in promoting national prosperity; and to all historical students should be full of interest. Some materials at least, for this unwritten chapter of British history are here supplied.'

VOL. I. throws some light upon the objects and extent of Inclosures, and the 4,120 Acts which brought about this great change in rural England. Among other subjects treated are the statutory history of Canals, Railways, Tramways, Gas-works, and Electric Lighting; Origin and Development of Royal and Parliamentary Jurisdiction in Private Bills; Ancient Precedents, in the quaint language of the originals; Parliamentary Divorce, Separation Bills for Cruelty of Husbands (cases of Lady Anglesea and Lady Ferrers); the Townshend Peerage Case; Bills for Attainder and Restitution in Blood, Naturalisation, &c.

VOL. II. (concluding the work) will appear in November.

London: BUTTERWORTHS, Fleet Street.

To show the influence we have in forwarding the interests of Advertisers, it may be mentioned that we have the SOLE AGENCY of the Advertisement Pages of THIS REVIEW; also of the SATURDAY REVIEW, THE CHILD'S PICTORIAL, The Calendar of the Incorporated Law Society, Charities Register and Digest (*Charity Organisation Society*), besides constantly retaining the BEST POSITIONS in many other important papers and books.

TIME, Labour, and Money may be saved by sending all announcements for Newspapers, Magazines, &c., through

HART'S ADVERTISING OFFICES. By a SINGLE ORDER an Advertisement can be inserted in any number of Papers, Religious or General. The Advertiser thus saves immense time and labour, and receives only ONE Advertising Account instead of one from each paper.

ANNOUNCEMENTS of Schools, Colleges, Societies, Memorial and other Public Funds, inserted (at Publishers' rates) in *Guardian, Church Times, Record, Times, Standard, Morning Post, Saturday Review, Spectator, Athenæum*, or any other paper in the world.

HART'S ADVERTISING OFFICES, 33 SOUTHAMPTON STREET, STRAND, LONDON, W.C.

PARTRIDGE & COOPER,

191 & 192 FLEET STREET, and 1 & 2 CHANCERY LANE, LONDON,

WHOLESALE AND RETAIL
MANUFACTURING STATIONERS.

The Royal Courts Note Paper,

The best *low-priced* Paper ever offered to the Public. Specimens and prices free on application.

DIE SINKING AND COLOUR STAMPING at half the usual prices.
NO CHARGE FOR PLAIN STAMPING *BEST PAPER & ENVELOPES.*

THE 'FACILE' SAFETY BICYCLE.
(BEALE & STRAW'S PATENT.)

The 'FACILE' is incomparably the best roadster ever introduced, whether for elderly or athletic riders, being Safe, Speedy, Comfortable, and Easy to learn, &c. During 1884 ten records of over 260 miles in one day have been made on the road, including Mr. Adams's ride of 266½ miles in one day, which beats all previous records on any Machine.

DESCRIPTIVE PAMPHLET FREE.

Sole Manufacturers—ELLIS & Co. Ld.
47 Farringdon Road, London, E.C.

ESTABLISHED 1851.

BIRKBECK BANK.—Southampton Buildings, Chancery Lane. Current Accounts opened according to the usual practice of other Bankers, and Interest allowed on the minimum monthly balances when not drawn below £50. No commission charged for keeping accounts.

The Bank also receives money on Deposit at Three per cent. Interest, repayable on demand.

The Bank undertakes for its Customers, free of charge, the custody of Deeds, Writings, and other Securities and Valuables; the Collection of Bills of Exchange, Dividends, and Coupons; and the purchase and sale of Stocks and Shares. Letters of Credit and Circular Notes issued. A Pamphlet on application.

FRANCIS RAVENSCROFT, *Manager.*

CRAMER'S NEW PIANOFORTES,

WITH IRON FRAMES.

J. B. CRAMER & CO. beg to call attention to their New Iron-framed Cottage Pianofortes, which combine great power and purity of tone, with a general excellence hitherto the characteristic of only the best Grand Pianofortes.

These Instruments are made in different sizes and cases, to meet the taste of all purchasers, and are supplied on Cramer's three years system, which, though partially adopted by others, is carried out on a thoroughly large and liberal scale only by themselves.

IRON-FRAMED PIANETTES	**From 30 Guineas.**
From £2. 16s. per quarter on their three years' system.	
IRON-FRAMED PIANINOS	**From 36 Guineas.**
From £3. 10s. per quarter on their three years' system.	
IRON-FRAMED COTTAGES	**From 55 Guineas.**
From £5. 5s. per quarter on their three years' system.	

FULL PARTICULARS POST FREE ON APPLICATION.

Nothing supplied but what is of the highest and most satisfactory quality. Exchanged any time within Six Months without loss to the Purchaser.

J. B. CRAMER & CO.,

Regent Street, W.; Bond Street, W.; High Street, Notting Hill, W.; Moorgate Street, E.C., LONDON. Church Street, LIVERPOOL. 20 West Street, and 88 Western Road, BRIGHTON. And of their Agents at DUBLIN, BELFAST, GLASGOW, and EDINBURGH; and the principal Musicsellers throughout the United Kingdom.

Scottish Provident Institution.

Edinburgh—6 ST. ANDREW SQUARE.   London Office—17 KING WILLIAM STREET, E.C.

At the 47th ANNUAL MEETING, on 25th MARCH, 1885,

THE DIRECTORS reported a satisfactory result of the year's business—the proposals received, £1,170,615. 10s., being somewhat above, while the amount accepted is somewhat under, those of last year. The New Assurances completed were £1,015,155; with Premiums, £35,274. Premiums received in Year, £482,840. Total Receipts, £688,920. Claims, £269,880. The Realised Funds (Increased in the Year by £327,540) amount to £5,063,835.

Only Two Offices in the Kingdom (both much older) have as large a Fund.

WHOLE-WORLD LICENCES AND NON-FORFEITURE OF POLICIES.

POLICIES are generally now free from restrictions on residence after five years, and unchallengeable on any ground but fraud.

POLICIES may be revived (after month of grace) on payment of premium within a year without proof of health. In case of death intervening, when the value exceeds the unpaid premium, the full sum is payable, under deduction of arrears.

The CHAIRMAN briefly referred to his early connection with the office, and as illustrating the advantage of Assuring early, particularly on a scale of Terminable Premiums, and as showing the Prosperity of the Institution, he instanced his own Policy as one of those which had been doubled, while he had paid no Premiums under it for many years.

The ADVANTAGES which this Institution offers are :—

A Larger Original Assurance—say £1,200 or £1,250 for the Premium charged elsewhere (with Profits) for £1,000 only.

The Prospect to Good Lives of Large Additions—no share being given to those by whose early death there is a loss.

Policies 'sharing a first time at last Investigation (1880) had additions of from 17 and 18 to upwards of 30 per cent., so that Assurances of £1,000 were increased to sums ranging from £1,170 to £1,300. Policies which shared at previous Investigations have been increased to £1,400, £1,700, and upwards.

Claims are payable One Month after proof of Death.

Reports, with full information, may be had on application.

J. MUIR LEITCH, *London Secretary.*   JAMES WATSON, *Manager.*

BRITISH EQUITABLE ASSURANCE COMPANY,

4 QUEEN STREET PLACE, E.C.

CAPITAL—A QUARTER OF A MILLION STERLING.

Directors.

WILLIAM MACDONALD BASDEN, Esq., Great St. Helen's, Bishopsgate Street, City, and Lloyd's.
GEORGE THOMAS DALE, Esq., Bayswater.
WILLIAM SUTTON GOVER, Esq., Casino House, Herne Hill, and 4 Queen Street Place, City.

JOHN MIDDLETON HARE, Esq., Stoke Newington.
FOUNTAIN JOHN HARTLEY, Esq., Clapton.
WILLIAM GEORGE LEMON, Esq., Lincoln's Inn.
WILLIAM SMITH, Esq., Upper Norwood.
EDWARD BEAN UNDERHILL, Esq., LL.D., Hampstead.

Auditors.

ALFRED HENRY BAYNES, Esq., Wandsworth. | JAMES CLARKE, Esq., Fleet Street, City.
WILLIAM POTTER OLNEY, Esq., New Kent Road,.

Solicitors.—Messrs. HENRY GOVER & SON, 3 Adelaide Place, London Bridge.
Bankers.—THE LONDON AND WESTMINSTER BANK, Lothbury.
Managing Director and Actuary.—WILLIAM SUTTON GOVER, Esq., F.S.S., F.I.A.
Assistant Actuary.—FREDERIC FIELD GOVER, Esq.
Sub-Manager.—JOHN WILKINSON FAIREY, Esq.

TWENTY-NINTH ANNUAL REPORT, MAY, 1884.

NEW BUSINESS.

2,097 Policies issued for £411,099
New Premium Income 12,566

BUSINESS IN FORCE.

26,704 Policies, assuring £4,943,145

REVENUE OF THE YEAR.

Premiums £144,626
Interest, &c. 37,695
                                                                £182,321

ACCUMULATED FUND.

Laid by in the year £65,507
Accumulated Fund on 31st January, 1884 (equal to 76 per cent. of the net premiums received upon Policies in force.. .. .. £938,600

ACCUMULATED FUND AT END OF DECEMBER, 1884, EXCEEDS ONE MILLION STERLING.

Claims and Bonuses paid under Company's Policies £800,803
Average Reversionary Bonus for 27 years, about 1¼ per cent. per annum.

MISSION BUILDINGS FUND
OF THE
INCORPORATED CHURCH BUILDING SOCIETY.

'England is now a vast Mission Field, half filled with home heathen.'—BISHOP OF WINCHESTER, Church Congress, 1879.

MISSION BUILDINGS ARE URGENTLY NEEDED—

1. In Towns, as Chapels-of-Ease, or as nurseries to the Mother Church, for less formal services, addresses by laymen, &c.
2. In Hamlets, for the young, the feeble, and the aged.
3. In New Districts. Some of the best known London Churches thus began their work.

'In many districts, the only way to establish a church is by first getting together a congregation in a Mission hall.'—(The late) CANON MILLER.

4. For Special Classes, navvies, sailors, &c. They are economical and attractive.

'A good church with a certain number of Mission chapels would more economically do the work of the Church.'—EARL NELSON.

The Society has already made grants towards 460 Mission buildings, amounting to £12,328. Many applications have to be deferred from lack of means.
Will Churchpeople contribute to aid this effort on behalf of one of the greatest needs of the Church at the present time?
At nearly every meeting of the Committee all the money in hand is voted away.
CONTRIBUTIONS will be gratefully received by the Rev. R. MILBURN BLAKISTON, 2 Dean's Yard, London, S.W.

Marriage Law Defence Union.

THE Bill for legalising Marriage with a Deceased Wife's Sister, which this year, as last, was strangely intercepted in the House of Lords by a Ministerial crisis, is not to be brought on again there this Session. But the Parliamentary lull is no holiday to the MARRIAGE LAW DEFENCE UNION. It is during such periods of rest that public opinion can be educated and the means of defence organised. It is necessary for the usefulness, if not for the very existence, of the Union, that it should keep itself conspicuously and continuously before the public, by way of advertisements and publications, large or small, dissecting the question in all its aspects.

These operations involve a continual drain of ready money, and the Union has only the free-will offerings of right-minded persons to look to for means of resisting the lavish expenditure of persons directly interested in promoting a change in the law. If these fail the Society must languish, and for any consequent failure of the cause those who hold back from helping to fight the battle will be responsible.

An earnest appeal is now made to all who desire to maintain the ancient standard of purity and the happy family life secured by our old marriage law, to come forward and testify, by the liberality of their gift, that they appreciate the services of the MARRIAGE LAW DEFENCE UNION, and desire to help in its labours.

Cheques &c. should be crossed HERRIES & Co. *or* GLYN & Co., *and made payable to* G. J. MURRAY.
20 COCKSPUR STREET, S.W., *June* 1885.

SUMMER APPEAL on BEHALF of
MISSION TO DEEP SEA FISHERMEN.

FOUR Mission Vessels cruise with the North Sea Trawling Fleets, but *eight more* are needed. Each Vessel is fitted specially for this service, and is at once a church, dispensary, library, and club.

'They are doing a grand work, worthy of the support of a great maritime nation like England,' were the words of the chairman of the International Fisheries Exhibition, Mr. Edward Birkbeck, M.P.

The 12,000 Smacksmen, who toil through furious blast and sleety storm, who hazard their lives, and fall victims—hundreds of them—to the pitiless waves in order that our tables may be supplied with fish, *may rightly claim some small share in the privileges we so richly enjoy and so highly prize.* THIS THEY CAN ONLY HAVE BY MEANS OF THESE MISSION VESSELS, carrying to the fishermen the message of Divine mercy and love, bringing the pleasure of books to while away the weary hours, affording relief in case of sickness and injury, and cheering and brightening dull and monotonous lives by their presence and ministry. Ladies may help by knitting cuffs; but help in money is sorely and largely needed. *Who will liberally aid in placing a Mission Vessel with every Trawling Fleet?*

E. J. MATHER, *Secretary.*
31 NEW BRIDGE STREET, LUDGATE CIRCUS, E.C.

*It is to the Pen what the Sewing Machine is to the Needle!
No Office or Library complete without it!*

THE REMINGTON STANDARD TYPE-WRITER.

CAPITALS and small letters.

No. 2 Type Writer £21.

A MACHINE to supersede the pen for manuscript writing, correspondence, &c., having twice the speed of a pen; is always ready for use, simple in construction, not liable to get out of order, easily understood. It is used in Government Offices, by Merchants, Bankers, Lawyers, Clergymen, Doctors, Scientists, &c. &c.

The writing is done by touching keys, and the manipulation is so simple and easy that anyone who can spell can write with it. It prints several styles of type, including capitals and small letters.

CORRESPONDENCE.—The merchant, the banker, *all* men of business, can perform the labour of letter-writing with much saving of valuable time. By using a copying-ink ribbon, very beautiful copies may be taken in the usual manner in the letter-press.

EDITORS and AUTHORS.—For writers for the press it is an almost incalculable benefit; as, in addition to its *saving of time* and *money* by its *perfect legibility*, 'clean proof' is secured, and they are also enabled to see how their thoughts will look in print before they are sent to press.

ITS ADVANTAGES OVER THE PEN.

LEGIBILITY.—The writing of this machine is fully as legible as print, and nearly as uniform and beautiful; the vexatious mistakes, annoyances, and waste of time incidental to illegible pen writing are therefore avoided.

RAPIDITY.—The average speed of the pen is from fifteen to thirty words a minute. The average speed of the Type-Writer is from fifty to seventy words a minute. Thus ten hours' work with the pen can be done by the Type-Writer in five hours, one good operator on the machine being fully equal to two expert penmen.

EASE.—As the operator on the machine can write with any finger of either hand, and can sit in any desired position, it is manifest that the drudgery of writing with the pen, whereby a *single set of muscles* is used, and a constrained position of the body necessitated, is overcome. No fear of pen paralysis, loss of sight, or curvature of the spine, from using the machine.

'I have worked the machine for eight consecutive hours without more than ten minutes' interruption, and at the end of that time my hands were not conscious of the least fatigue.
    R. BRUDENELL CARTER, F.R.C.S., &c.'

CAPITALS ONLY.

No. 4 Type-Writer, £18.

BEEMAN AND ROBERTS,
Sole Agents for the United Kingdom,
6 KING STREET, CHEAPSIDE, LONDON, E.C.

FURTHER PARTICULARS FREE ON APPLICATION OR BY POST.

TWO GOLD MEDALS 'THE HEALTHERIES,' 1884.

THOMAS BRADFORD & CO., LAUNDRY AND DAIRY ENGINEERS,
140 to 143 High Holborn, London;
Victoria St., Manchester; Bold St., Liverpool;
and Crescent Iron Works, Salford.

The Many Laundries,—of almost every capacity, both for—Hand Power,—Steam Power.—Gas Power,—Water Power,—that we have during the last twenty-five years fitted up almost everywhere,—have uniformly been satisfactory in their results—those of recent years more especially so. Economy,—and a perfect and thorough system of cleansing and purifying all sorts of linen,—more especially *body* linen,—so essential to bodily health,—are absolutely ensured.

Consultation by appointment;—every class of Laundry can be inspected in operation,—complete plans furnished when required,—as required—for House, Mansion, School, Hotel, Workhouse, Asylum, Hospital, or Steam Laundry.

General Catalogue free by post.

Our Model Dairy Fittings consist of 'Diaphragm' Barrel and 'Declivity' Box Churns, 'Albany' and 'Springfield' Butter Workers, Revolving-Disc Milk Pan Stands, to which some 40 Gold and Silver Medals have been awarded. See special Dairy Catalogue (which is very comprehensive), free by post.

A LUXURY TO ALL READERS.

For holding a Book or writing desk, lamp, meals, &c., in any position over an easy chair, bed, or sofa.
PRICES from £1. 1s.

BATH CHAIRS 30s

Self-Propelling Chairs, **£4. 10s.**
Carrying Chairs, From **£1. 5s.**
Bed Table from **10s.**

JOHN CARTER, 6a, New Cavendish St.,
Portland Place, London, W.—Only Address.
ILLUSTRATED PRICE LISTS (68 PAGES) POST FREE.
GOLD MEDAL,
HEALTH EXHIBITION.
TELEPHONE No. 3881.

HAY FEVER & COLDS
CURED BY **DR. DUNBAR'S** CURED BY
ALKARAM
2/9 EACH. **SMELLING BOTTLE,** 2/9 EACH.

Which, if inhaled on the first symptoms, will at once remove them, and even when a cold has been neglected and become severe, it will give immediate relief, and generally cure in one day. To open the Bottle, dip the stopper into very hot water, and rub off the isinglass.

Address Dr. DUNBAR, care of F. NEWBERY & SONS, 1 King Edward Street, Newgate Street, St. Paul's London.

MILES DOUGHTY'S
VOICE LOZENGE,
FOR SINGERS, FOR SPEAKERS,
RECITERS, &c.

SING WELL! SPEAK WELL!—*Doughty's Voice Lozenge* has been gratefully appreciated by thousands of clerical, musical, and other celebrities for nearly 40 years. It imparts to the voice clearness of sound and brilliancy of tone.

JENNY LIND.—'I have much pleasure in confirming, as far as my experience extends, the testimony already so general in favour of the Lozenge prepared by you' (Miles Doughty).

6d., 1s., 2s. 6d., 5s. and 11s.—post free, 7d., 1s. 2d. &c.
Ask your Chemist for them.—F. NEWBERY & SONS, 1 King Edward Street, London, E.C. Established A.D. 1746.

BELL'S
SECRETE OIL
(REGISTERED).

The best, cheapest, and most wholesome hair preparation. It does not clog, and is *not* a dye.

BELL'S
UNIQUE
VEGETABLE EXTRACT
(REGISTERED).
Is an astringent hair-dressing. It cleanses the scalp effectually.

Prices of OIL or EXTRACT. 1/, 2/, 5/.
By Post 1/3, 2/3, or 5/3.
F. NEWBERY & SONS, Sole Proprietors, 1 King Edward St., Newgate St. London. *Established over 40 Years.*

HIMROD'S CURE FOR ASTHMA

The Discoverer of HIMROD'S CURE, who was for Twelve Years a great sufferer with that terrible disease, Asthma, has, after many trials and failures, at last succeeded in bringing together a combination which is now offered to the public with the fullest confidence in its value AS A CURE. It has been thoroughly tested in many of the worst cases, and all conversant with its merits unite in awarding to it the most unqualified praise.

Of all Chemists. 4s. per box, or, by remitting 4s. 3d. to the undersigned, a box will be mailed to any address, charges paid.
F. NEWBERY & SONS,
(British Depot) 1 King Edward Street, Newgate Street, London, E.C.

POOLE & LORD,

318 (late 145) OXFORD STREET,

OUTFITTERS, NEARLY OPPOSITE BOND STREET, W.

SOLE INVENTORS OF THE SANS-PLIS SHIRT. HOSIERS, AND GLOVERS.

In correspondence with

ASQUITH & LORD, 8 Rampart Row Bombay.

The SANS-PLIS Shirt is superior to any other for Indian and Colonial wear. Being entirely free from gathers, it is cooler, much stronger, and will bear the Indian mode of washing better than any other Shirt in use.

A single Shirt, or other article, made to *measure*, and accurate patterns preserved to ensure correctness in the execution of future orders.

AMERICAN WHISKY.

RARE OLD, FINEST QUALITY, 48s. per DOZEN CASE.

Forwarded CARRIAGE PAID to any Railway Station in the United Kingdom on receipt of remittance for above amount.

JAMES SMITH & CO.,
WINE MERCHANTS,

LIVERPOOL,	9 LORD STREET.
MANCHESTER,	26 MARKET STREET.
BIRMINGHAM,	83 HIGH STREET.

BECKETT'S FRUIT DRINKS

Analytical Report from GEORGE BOSTOCK, Esq., F.C.S., F.A.S., Manchester:—"BECKETT'S BEVERAGES' are perfectly pure and free from anything deleterious to health; they are non-intoxicating, and form pleasant and invigorating drinks. The *Lime-Fruit Syrup, Black Currant, Raspberry, Lemon, Orange, &c.*, make capital summer drinks, mixed with either plain or aërated water. All kinds except Tonics, Pints 1s. 9d. (sufficient for 20 tumblers), Half-pints 1s. Orange and Quinine, Pints 3/-, ½-pints 1/9; Lime and Quinine and Hops, Pints 2/3, ½-pints 1/3.

☞ Should there be any difficulty in procuring any of the above, write to the Manufacturer, W. BECKETT, Heywood, MANCHESTER, who will send Two Pints and upwards to any address, carriage paid, on receipt of P.O.O. Sold by Chemists, Grocers, and Coffee Tavern Co.'s.

JOSEPH GILLOTT'S STEEL PENS.

GOLD MEDAL,   PARIS, 1878.

ART FURNITURE.
ADAMS DESIGNS.
CHIPPENDALE.

MAPLE & CO.
Tottenham Court Road.

TURKEY CARPETS.
INDIAN CARPETS.
PERSIAN CARPETS.

MAPLE & CO., Upholsterers by Special Appointment to Her Majesty.—The LARGEST FURNISHING ESTABLISHMENT in the World. Acres of Show Rooms for the display of every description of household requisites.

MAPLE & CO., Timber Merchants and Direct Importers of the finest Woods to be found in Africa, Asia, and America, and Manufacturers of Cabinet Furniture in various woods by steam-power.

MAPLE & CO.—YEW TREE WOOD FURNITURE. This is the most fashionable novelty, somewhat resembling mahogany in colour, but much lighter and brighter looking, and suitable for bedrooms. The price is about the same as for mahogany.

MAPLE & CO. — SEQUOIA, Oregon Woods, Circassian Ash, Hungarian Ash, Satin-Wood, and American Walnut, all made very strong and durable FURNITURE. These woods are all to be seen in their manufactured state.

MAPLE & CO.—Bass Wood FURNITURE is one of the novelties particularly recommended, being much harder than pine, and a prettier wood. 500 Bedroom Suites, finished in various woods, to select from. Prices from 5½ to 250 guineas. Many of these are quite novelties in shape and finish.

500 BEDROOM SUITES on Show to select from. Established 48 years.

TURKEY CARPETS.—MAPLE & CO. have just received large consignments of fine TURKEY CARPETS, unique colourings, reproductions of the 17th century, being the first delivery of those made from this season's clip.—MAPLE & CO., London, and 17 and 18 Local Baron Aliotti, Smyrna.

TURKEY CARPETS. — These special Carpets are exceptionally fine, both in colour and quality, while the prices are lower than ever known before. Appended are a few examples of useful sizes, with prices. The trade supplied :—
11 ft. 4 in. by 8 ft. 3 in. £6 10 0
12 ft. 0 in. by 10 ft. 6 in. 7 15 0
13 ft. 0 in. by 11 ft. 9 in. 8 10 0
14 ft. 9 in. by 11 ft. 0 in. 9 15 0
15 ft. 0 in. by 11 ft. 10 in. 11 15 0

WOODSTOCK CARPETS.—These are inexpensive, but most artistic productions of the English loom, woven in one piece, without seam, bordered and fringed, suitable for reception and bedrooms. Can be had in many sizes.
8ft. 0in. × 7ft. 6in. £0 19 6 | 12ft. 0in. × 10ft. 6in. £2 1 0
9ft. 0in. × 7ft. 6in. 1 2 0 | 12ft. (in. × 12ft. 0in. 2 6 6
9ft. 0in. × 9ft. 0in. 1 8 3 | 13ft. 6in. × 10ft. 6in. 2 6 0
10ft. 8in. × 9ft. 0in. 1 10 6 | 13ft. 6in. × 12ft. 0in. 2 12 6
10ft. 6in. × 10ft. 6in. 1 15 9 | 15ft. 0in. × 12ft. 0in. 2 18 6
12ft. 6in. × 9ft. 0in. 1 15 0 | Rugs to match, 6ft. × 3ft. 6/6
Several hundreds of old patterns at reduced prices. Each Carpet is protected by the Trade Mark, 'Woodstock.' Can only be had of MAPLE & CO., Carpet Factory. Purchasers of Fringed Carpets should beware of imitations.

BEDSTEADS.
BEDSTEADS.
BEDSTEADS.

MAPLE & CO.
LONDON.

NEW SHOW ROOMS.
NEW SHOW ROOMS.
NEW SHOW ROOMS.

MAPLE & CO. have seldom less than 10,000 BEDSTEADS in stock, comprising some 700 various patterns, in sizes from 2 ft. 6 in. to 5 ft. 6 in. wide, ready for immediate delivery—on the day of purchase, if desired. The disappointment and delay incident to choosing from designs only, where but a limited stock is kept, is thus avoided. Catalogues Free.

MAPLE & CO.—300 BRASS and IRON BEDSTEADS, fitted with Bedding complete in Show Rooms, to select from. Strong Iron Bedsteads from 6s. 6d. to 10 guineas; Brass Bedsteads from 70s. to 40 guineas. 10,000 in stock.

MAPLE & CO. have a SPECIAL DEPARTMENT for IRON and BRASS Four-post BEDSTEADS, Cribs, and Cots, specially adapted for mosquito curtains, used in India, Australia, and the Colonies. Price for full-sized Bedsteads, varying from 25s. Shippers and Colonial visitors are invited to inspect this varied stock, the largest in England, before deciding elsewhere. 10,000 Bedsteads to select from.

MAPLE & CO.
SPRING MATTRESSES.

MAPLE & CO.
HAIR MATTRESSES.

MAPLE & CO.
Wire-Woven MATTRESSES.

MAPLE & CO.—Spring Mattresses.— The PATENT Wire-woven SPRING MATTRESS. Such advantageous arrangements have been made that this much-admired Mattress is sold at the following low prices :—3 ft., 15s. 9d.; 3 ft. 6 in., 18s. 9d.; 4 ft., 21s. 6d.; 4 ft. 6 in., 24s. 6d.

POSTAL ORDER DEPARTMENT.— Messrs. MAPLE & CO. beg respectfully to state that this Department is now so organised that they are fully prepared to execute and supply any article that can possibly be required in Furnishing at the same price, if not less, than any other horse in England. Patterns sent and quotations given free of charge.

MAPLE & CO., Tottenham Court Road, London,
And Boulevard de Strasburg, Paris.

MAPLE & CO.—The Specimen Rooms are good examples of high-class DECORATIVE FURNISHING, carried out in perfect taste, without extravagant expenditure. Every one about to Furnish, or re-arrange their residences, would derive information by an inspection.

MAPLE & CO.'S FURNISHING ESTABLISHMENT, the largest in the World. Acres of Show Rooms for the display of first-class Furniture, ready for immediate delivery. Novelties every day from all parts of the globe. No family ought to furnish before viewing this collection of household requisites, it being one of the sights in London. To Export Merchants an unusual advantage is offered. Having large space, all goods are packed on the premises by experienced packers.

NEW ILLUSTRATED CATALOGUE FREE.

DECORATIONS, Artistic Wall Papers.— Messrs. MAPLE & CO. undertake every description of ARTISTIC HOUSE DECORATION, including gas-fitting, repairs, parquet work, &c. The head of this Department is a thoroughly qualified architect, assisted by a large staff of artists and skilled workmen. Coloured Drawings and Estimates furnished.

MAPLE & CO. 400-DAY CLOCKS.

MAPLE & CO. Dining-room CLOCKS.

MAPLE & CO. Drawing-room CLOCKS.

MAPLE & CO. — DRAWING - ROOM CLOCKS to go for 400 days with once winding; a handsome present. Price 70s., warranted. MAPLE & CO. have a large and varied assortment suitable for Dining and Drawing-room. Over 500 to select from. Prices from 10s. 9d. Handsome Marble Clock, with incised lines in gold, and superior eight-day movement, 23s. 6d.; also Bronzes in great variety.

THE CLOCK, Bronze, and Ornamental China DEPARTMENT comprises a choice selection of Dresden, Sèvres, Worcester, Derby, Coalport, Minton, Doulton, Hungarian, and Oriental China. The largest and most varied collection in the world.—MAPLE & CO., London.

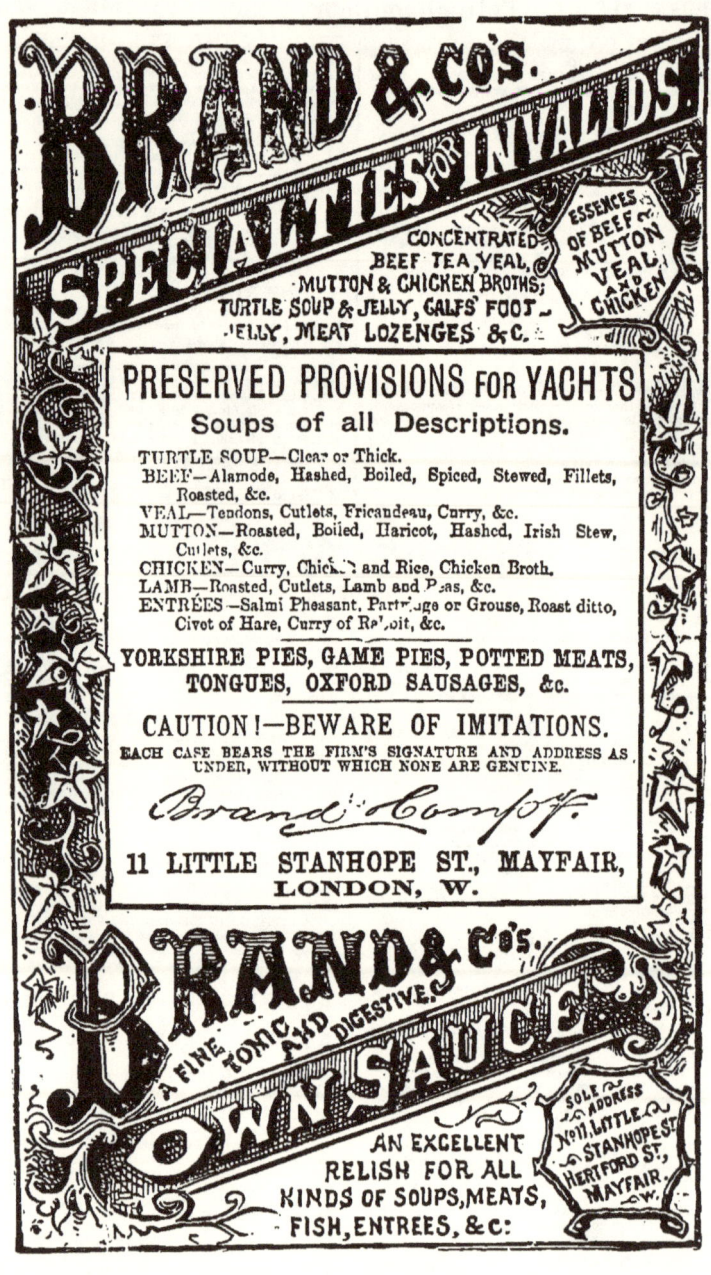

FURNISH THROUGHOUT. (Regd.)
OETZMANN & CO.
67, 69, 71, 73, 77 & 79,
HAMPSTEAD ROAD,
NEAR TOTTENHAM COURT ROAD, LONDON.

ORDERS PER POST RECEIVE PROMPT AND FAITHFUL ATTENTION.

DWARF SUTHERLAND, OR SMALL FIVE O'CLOCK TEA TABLE.
Unpolished .... 15s. 6d.
Walnut, Polished or Ebonised .... 17s. 6d.
Ditto, Black and Gold .... 21s. 0d.
Large size Mahogany ditto. measures about 3ft. by 3ft. when opened, £2. 5s. 6d.

BLACK AND GOLD OR WALNUT AND GOLD DECORATED CORNER BRACKET,
8s. 9d.
Post-free, 9d. extra.

OCCASIONAL EASY CHAIRS,
Upholstered in Rich Silk Tapestries and Plush, with Carved Banisters, or stuffed at back, 28s. 6d.
An immense variety of Easy Chairs always on view in the Showrooms.

ILLUSTRATED AND DESCRIPTIVE CATALOGUES POST FREE.

Factory Founded A.D. 1735.

WALKDEN'S

WRITING AND COPYING INKS.

WALKDEN'S EXTRA BLACK INK.
WALKDEN'S BLUE-BLACK WRITING FLUID.
WALKDEN'S BLUE-BLACK COPYING FLUID.
WALKDEN'S SCARLET INK for STEEL PENS.

These celebrated Inks are prepared with great care from the purest materials, and are adapted to the wants of all writers.

OF ALL STATIONERS THROUGHOUT GREAT BRITAIN & COLONIES.

SOLE MANUFACTURERS:
COOPER & CO., 5, 6, & 7 SHOE LANE, LONDON.

HEAL & SON.

BEDSTEADS.—3 ft. IRON FRENCH, from 10s. 6d. 3 ft. BRASS FRENCH, from 48s.
BEDDING.—MATTRESSES, 3 ft., from 11s. A NEW SPRING MATTRESS, warranted good and serviceable, 3 ft., 28s.; 4 ft. 6 in., 40s.
HEAL'S PATENT SOMMIER ELASTIQUE PORTATIF, of which 30,000 have been sold, is the best Spring Mattress yet invented. 3 ft., 40s.; 5 ft., 63s. This, with a French Mattress, makes a most luxurious bed.

BEDROOM FURNITURE.—PLAI[N] SUITES, from £3. DECORATED SUITES, fro[m] £8. 10s.
SUITES OF WHITE ENAMEL, similar to that in the Health Exhibition, from £14.
ASH AND WALNUT SUITES, from £12s. 12s.
SCREENS, suitable for Bedrooms, 21s.
EASY CHAIRS, from 35s. COUCHES, from 75s.

ILLUSTRATED CATALOGUE, with PRICE LIST OF BEDDING, FREE BY POST.

195 to 198 TOTTENHAM COURT ROAD.

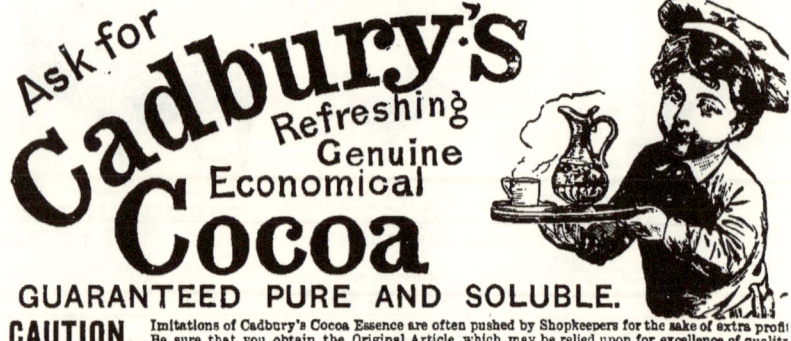

Ask for **Cadbury's** Refreshing Genuine Economical **Cocoa**

GUARANTEED PURE AND SOLUBLE.

CAUTION. Imitations of Cadbury's Cocoa Essence are often pushed by Shopkeepers for the sake of extra profit. Be sure that you obtain the Original Article, which may be relied upon for excellence of quality, purity, and strength. **MAKERS TO THE QUEEN.**

Allen & Hanburys "Perfected" COD-LIVER OIL

'Is as nearly tasteless as Cod-Liver Oil can be.'—*Lancet.*
'Has almost the delicacy of salad oil.'—*Brit. Med. Journal.*
'No nauseous eructations follow after it is swallowed.'—*Medical Press.*

It can be borne and digested by the most delicate; is the only oil which does not 'repeat'; and for these reasons the most efficacious kind in use. In capsuled bottles only, at 1s. 4d., 2s. 6d., 4s. 9d., and 9s. **Sold everywhere.**

Allen & Hanburys' MALT EXTRACT Forms a valuable adjunct to Cod-Liver Oil. Highly concentrated and nutritious. A powerful aid to digestion. It can be obtained through any Chemist. In Bottles at 2s. and 3s. 6d.

Pears Soap

Recommended (in the Journal of Cutaneous Medicine) by

Professor SIR ERASMUS WILSON, LL.D., F.R.S.,

President of the Royal College of Surgeons, Eng.

1885. AGENTS FOR MELNOTTE ET FILS' REIMS CHAMPAGNE.

BY APPOINTMENT TO
HER MAJESTY
AND THE
ROYAL FAMILY.

ORIGINALLY
ESTABLISHED
A.D. 1667.

Registered Telegraphic Address: HEDGES BUTLER.
Telephone 3809.

HEDGES & BUTLER,
Wine Shippers and Merchants,

SPAIN:	LONDON:	BRIGHTON:
SHIPPING CELLARS AT	CHIEF OFFICE AND CELLARS,	CELLARS,
JEREZ-DE-LA-FRONTERA.	155 REGENT STREET.	30 KING'S ROAD.

BONDED STORES, CRESCENT VAULT, LONDON DOCKS, E.

DUTY PAID.   HOME LIST.

Shipped direct from **HEDGES & BUTLER'S** Shipping Cellars at Jerez-de-la-Frontera, Spain.

SHERRY.	Per Doz.	Per Octave, 13½ Gals. or 6 Doz.9 Bots.	Per Qr.-Cask, 27 Gals. or 13½ Doz.	Per Hhd., 54 Gals. or 27 Doz.	Per Butt, 108 Gals. or 54 Doz.	Mark and Brand.
Natural, or Val de Peñas	18/-	£6 0	£11 0	£20 10	£41	1 Val de Peñas
Pale	20/-	£6 5	£12 0	£23 10	£46	2 V. P.
Old Pale	24/-	£7 10	£14 10	£28 0	£55	3
„ Gold	24/-	£7 10	£14 10	£28 0	£55	4 Montes
„ Pale Dry	30/-	£9 10	£18 10	£36 0	£70	5 P.S.P.
Old Golden	30/-	£9 10	£18 10	£36 0	£70	6 S.P.
„ Brown	30/-	£9 10	£18 10	£36 0	£70	7 B.S.P.
Vino de Pasto (Mess Wine)	36/-	£11 5	£22 0	£43 0	£84	8 Pasto
Old Fashioned Gold	36/-	£11 5	£22 0	£43 0	£84	9 M.A.
„ Brown	36/-	£11 5	£22 0	£43 0	£84	10 B.M.A.
Manzanilla, Light	36/-	£11 5	£22 0	£43 0	£84	11 Manzanilla 1
Fine Old Dry	42/-	£13 5	£25 10	£50 0	£98	12 Peninsula
„ „ Golden	42/-	£13 5	£25 10	£50 0	£98	13 Albion
„ „ Brown	42/-	£13 5	£25 10	£50 0	£98	14 Emerald
Manzanilla	42/-	£13 5	£25 10	£50 0	£98	15 Manzanilla 2
Montilla	42/-	£13 5	£25 10	£50 0	£98	16 Montilla 1
Fine Old Natural (recommended for Invalids)	42/-	£13 5	£25 10	£50 0	£98	17 Old Natural
Superior Old Amontillado (Club)	48/-	£15 0	£29 0	£57 0	£112	18 Amontillado 1
„ Pale Dry	48/-	£15 0	£29 0	£57 0	£112	19 P.D.S.
„ East India, Golden (Shipped round the World)	48/-	£15 0	£29 0	£57 0	£112	20 Blanche
„ Brown	48/-	£15 0	£29 0	£57 0	£112	21 Palmers
„ Montilla	48/-	£15 0	£29 0	£57 0	£112	22 Montilla 2
„ Manzanilla	48/-	£15 0	£29 0	£57 0	£112	23 Manzanilla 2
Choice Delicate Amontillado	54/-	£17 10	£32 0	£65 0	£124	24 Amontillado 3
„ Deep Golden	54/-	£17 10	£32 0	£65 0	£124	25 Lansdowne
Very Superior Amontillado	60/-	£18 15	£36 10	£69 0	£136	26 Amontillado 3
„ Old Pale	60/-	£18 15	£36 10	£69 0	£136	27 S.O.P.
„ Old Brown	60/-	£18 15	£36 10	£69 0	£136	28 Rambler
„ Montilla	60/-	£18 15	£36 10	£69 0	£136	29 Montilla 3
„ Manzanilla	60/-	£18 15	£36 10	£69 0	£136	30 Manzanilla 4
Extra Superior Old Amontillado Fino (as supplied to H.M. the King of Spain)	72/-	£22 10	£44 0	£85 0	£168	31 Rex Fino

Single Bottles of the above Wines supplied. For Wines and Spirits in Bond see Special Export List.

CHEQUES CROSSED : BANK OF ENGLAND.

[CONTINUED OVER.

HEDGES & BUTLER'S WINE LIST.

SHERRY.

	Per Doz.	Per Octave, 13½ Gals. or 6 Doz. 9 Bots.	Per Qr.-Cask. 27 Gals. or 13½ Doz.	Per Hhd., 54 Gals. or 27 Doz.	Per Butt, 108 Gals. or 54 Doz.
Extra Superior Old Brown East India Dessert (Shipped round the World ex "Star of Albion")	72/-	£22 10	£44 0	£85 0	£168
Extra Superior Oloroso	72/-	£22 10	£44 0	£85 0	£168
,, Amoroso	72/-	£22 10	£44 0	£85 0	£168
Choicest Old Golden	84/-	£26 0	£50 0	£98 0	£190
,, Amontillado	84/-	£26 0	£50 0	£96 0	£190
,, Old Bottled Amoroso	96/-	—	—	—	—
,, ,, Oloroso	96/-	—	—	—	—
Old Fashioned Golden	120/-	—	—	—	—
Fifty Years Old, Pale	144/-	—	—	—	—
,, Golden	144/-	—	—	—	—
,, Brown	144/-	—	—	—	—
Very Choice Old East India	144/-	—	—	—	—
Pedro Jimenez (a luscious Dessert Wine), many years in bottle	84/-	—	—	—	—
Paxerette	84/-	—	—	—	—
Malaga	60/-	—	—	—	—
Choicest Old Bottled ditto	84/-	—	—	—	—
Rota Tent (for Sacramental use)	42/-	—	—	—	—
Old Bottled Ditto	48/-	—	—	—	—

PORT (From the Wood).

	Per Doz.	Per Octave Cask, 6 Doz. 9 Bots.	Per Qr.-Cask, 13 Doz. 6 Bots.	Per Hhd., 27 Doz.	Per 57
Young, full body	24/-	£7 10	£14 10	£28 0	£
,, Fruity	30/-	£9 10	£18 10	£36 0	£
Dry Tawny (recommended for Invalids)	36/-	£11 5	£22 0	£43 0	£
Fruity	36/-	£11 5	£22 0	£43 0	£
Old Fruity	42/-	£13 5	£25 10	£50 0	£
Choice Old	48/-	£15 0	£29 0	£57 0	£1
Very Old Tawny	60/-	£18 15	£36 10	£69 0	£1
Vintage 1878, for laying down	48/-	£15 0	£29 0	£57 0	£1
,, 1881 (will be equal to 1834)	48/-	£15 0	£29 0	£57 0	£1

OLD BOTTLED PORT.

	Per Doz.	Per Doz. Hf.-Bots.	Mark and Brand.
Very Superior Old Crusted	42/-	23/-	10 ex "Ann"
,, ,, Older, in bottle	48/-	26/-	11 ,, "Jane"
,, ,, ,, ,,	54/-	29/-	12 ,, "Englishman"
,, ,, ,, ,,	60/-	32/-	13 ,, "Beeswing"
,, ,, ,, ,,	72/-	38/-	14 ,, "Tagus"
,, ,, ,, ,,	84/-	45/-	15 ,, "Lisbon"
Twenty years in bottle	96/-	—	16 —
Vintage 1858	120/-	—	17 1858
,, 1834	144/-	—	18 1834
Ventuzelo (very dry), "The Amontillado of the Douro"	96/-	—	19 VTO

SPARKLING RED BURGUNDY.

		Per Hhd., Per Doz. 23 Doz., Per Doz.	Hf.-Botts. Including Bottling.
1 Sparkling Red Burgundy		48/-	26/- —
2 ,, ,,		60/-	32/- —
3 ,, Corton		72/-	38/- —
4 ,, Clos-de-Vougeôt		84/-	44/- —

SPARKLING WHITE BURGUNDY.

Chablis and Pouilly	24/-	14/-
,, ,,	30/-	17/-
,, ,,	36/-	20/-
,, ,,	42/-	23/-
Montrachet	48/-	26/-
,,	60/-	32/-
St. Péray and Sparkling St. Péray	60/-	32/-
Sparkling White Burgundy	60/-72/-84/-	— —

RED BURGUNDY.

Beaujolais ....
 ,, Older in bottle...
Macon ....
Beaune ....
 ,, 1878..................
St. George ....
 ,, ...
Pommard ....
 ,, ...
Rousillon ....
 ,, ...
Very Old Rousillon, 10 years in bottle ....
Volnay (highly recommended)
 ,, Older in bottle ......
Chambertin ....
 ,, ...
Côte Rôtie ....
 ,, ...
Corton ....
 ,, ...
Nuits ....
 ,, ...
Romanée ....
 ,, ...
Richebourg ....
 ,, ...
Clos-de-Vougeôt ....
 ,, 1868 Vintage 1
Hermitage ....
 ,, ...

CHEQUES CROSSED: BANK OF ENGLAND.

HEDGES & BUTLER'S WINE LIST. 3

Per Doz.	Per Doz. Hf.-Bots.	Per Hhd., 23 Dzn., Including Bottling
.. 14/-	.. 9/-	...... £14
.. 18/-	.. 11/-	...... £18
.. 20/-	.. 12/-	...... £20
.. 24/-	.. 14/-	...... £24
.. 24/-	.. 14/-	...... £24
.. 30/-	.. 17/-	...... £30
.. 30/-	.. 17/-	...... £30
.. 36/-	.. 20/-	...... £36
.. 36/-	.. 20/-	...... £36
.. 42/-	.. 23/-	...... £42
.. 42/-	.. 23/-	...... £42
.. 42/-	.. 23/-	...... £42
.. 42/-	.. 23/-	...... £42
.. 48/-	.. 26/-	...... £48
.. 48/-	.. 26/-	...... £48
.. 48/-	.. 26/-	...... £48
.. 54/-	.. 29/-	...... £54
.. 54/-	.. 29/-	...... £54
.. 60/-	.. 32/-	...... £60
.. 60/-	.. 32/-	...... £60
.. 60/-	.. 32/-	...... £60
.. 72/-	.. 38/-	...... £72
.. 72/-	.. 38/-	...... £72
.. 72/-	.. 38/-	...... £72

84/-, 96/-, 120/-, 200/-,
Vintages 1868, 1869, 1870,
1873, 1874.

Per Doz. / Per Hhd. 23 Doz.
aying down)... 72/- £72

CHAMPAGNE.

	Per Doz.	Hf.-Bts.	Shipping Order for 15 doz. Per Doz.	Per Doz.
1 Sparkling	36/-	... 20/-	... 34/-	... 19/-
2 ,,	42/-	... 23/-	... 40/-	... 22/-
3 Crown	48/-	... 26/-	... 46/-	... 25/-
4 Très-sec (Mess and Ball Wine)	60/-	... 32/-	... 58/-	... 31/-
5 Crown H.&B.'Rich'	60/-	... 32/-	... 58/-	... 31/-
6 Dry Sillery	72/-	... 38/-	... 70/-	... 37/-
7 RichSilleryCreaming	72/-	... 38/-	... 70/-	... 37/-
8 H.&B.,finest quality	78/-	... 42/-	... 76/-	... 40/-
9 Extra Dry (cuvée de Réserve)	84/-	... 45/-	—	—
10 Extra Creaming (cuvée de Réserve)	84/-	... 45/-	... 82/-	... 43/-
11 Cuvée exceptionelle 'Brut'	96/-	... 52/-	... 94/-	... 49/-

AGENTS FOR

MELNOTTE ET FILS'

CHAMPAGNES.

CUVÉE DE RESÉRVE,

Vintage 1880, Extra Sec, Sec, or Brut, 84s. per Dozen bottles, 45s. per Dozen half-bottles.

1880 Champagne specially recommended, and will be equal to 1874 Vintage.

UX. Per Doz.	Per Doz. Hlf.-Bots.	Per Hhd., 23 Doz. Including Bottling
... 24/-	...... 14/-	...... £24
... 30/-	...... 17/-	...... £30
... 36/-	...... 20/-	...... £36
... 42/-	...... 23/-	...... £42
... 48/-	...... 26/-	...... £48
... 60/-	...... 32/-	...... £60
... 72/-	...... 38/-	...... £72
... 84/-	...... 44/-	...... £84
... { 96/- 108/- 120/- 200/- Vintages 1865, 1868, 1870		

MOSELLE.

	Per Doz.	
Still Moselle	... 24/-	... 30/-
Zeltingen	36/- ... 42/-	... 48/-
Brauneberg&Grünhausen	... 48/-	... 60/-
Muscatel	... 60/-	... 72/-
Scharzberg...............	... 72/-	... 84/-
Sparkling Moselle........	48/- ... 60/-	... 72/-
Sparkling Dry Moselle (Réserve Cuvée), extra dry	...	... 84/-

Per Aum, 15 doz., 3/- per doz. less.

Per Doz.
... 24/- ... 30/-
0/- ... 36/- ... 42/-
... 54/- ... 60/-
8/- ... 60/- ... 72/-
... 60/- ... 72/-
0/- ... 72/- ... 84/-
... 54/- ... 60/-
... 72/- ... 84/- Per Aum,
4/- ... 60/- ... 72/- 15 doz.,
                      3/- per doz.
... 72/- ... 84/-   less.
... ...120/-
...144/- ...200/-

8/- ... 60/- ... 72/-
... 48/- ... 60/-
... 48/- ... 60/-
8/- ... 60/- ... 72/-

VARIOUS.

	Per Doz.		
MADEIRA	36/- ... 48/-	... 60/-	... 72/-
East India Madeira	... 84/-	... 96/-	...120/-
Malmsey Madeira (in ½-bots.)	...	... 60/-	... 72/-
Bucellas	...	...	... 42/-
Rich and Dry Lisbon	...	...	... 42/-
RICH, or DRY MARSALA	... 20/-	... 24/-	... 30/-
Mountain and Malaga	...	... 60/-	... 72/-
Vidonia, Teneriffe and Calcavella...............	...	... 42/-	... 48/-
Hungarian	...	... 30/-	... 36/-
Vermuth	...	... 36/-	... 48/-
Lachrymæ Christie and Malvasi	...	... 72/-	... 84/-
TARRAGONA & CATALAN	... 18/-	... 20/-	... 24/-

Sack, Malmsey, Frontignau, Constantia, Lunel, Muscat-de-Rivesaltes, Rota Tent, Italian, and other Wines.

REGISTERED TELEGRAPHIC ADDRESS: HEDGES BUTLER.

[CONTINUED OVER.

SPIRITS.

	Per Doz.
PALE COGNAC BRANDY	44/-...48/-...60/-...72/-...84/
Champagne Brandy	84/-
Liqueur Brandy (30 yrs. old)	120/-
Brown Cognac	48/-...60/-...72/-
White Brandy	84/-
OLD SCOTCH WHISKEY, GLENLIVAT & HIGHLAND	42/-...48/-...54/-
OLD IRISH WHISKEY	42/-...48/-...54/-
OLD Scotch and Irish Whiskey in 13-gallon Casks, £13, £14. 10/-, £16. 10/-	
OLD Scotch and Irish Whiskey in 27-gallon Casks, £27, £30. 10/-, £34. 10/-	
American Bourbon Whiskey	54/-
Jamaica Rum	42/-...48/-...54/-
White Rum	60/-

SWEET & UNSWEETENED

GIN	30/-...36/-
Schiedam Hollands	36/-
Apricot Brandy	84/-
Orange "	72/-
Ginger "	60/-
Dantzic Cherry Brandy	72/-...84/-
Copenhagen Cherry Brandy	72/-
Spirits of Wine	66/-

LIQUEURS.

Maraschino di Zara.
Kümmel.
Amsterdam Curaçao.
White Curaçao.
Kirschenwasser.
Trappistine.
Absinthe Suisse.
Elixir de Spa.
Chartreuse, Yellow. Ditto Green.
Anisette de Bordeaux.
Amsterdamsche Anisette.
Bénédictine.
Badminton Cup.
Cherry Ratafia. Half en Half.

Eau-di-Vie de Dantzic.
Aqua d'Oro and Aqua d'Argent
Crème de Noyau (red and white
" Vanille.
" Thé.
Captain Jaques Punch.
Old Milk Punch.
Old Turtle Punch (as supplied to H.R.H. the Prince Wales).
Old Tokay.
Apricot, Orange, and Ginger Brandy.
Santa Maria de Jamaica.
Angostura, Orange, and Dutch Bitters.

HEDGES & BUTLER,

Wine Shippers and Merchants,

SPAIN:
SHIPPING CELLARS AT
JEREZ-DE-LA-FRONTERA.

LONDON:
CHIEF OFFICE AND CELLARS,
155 REGENT STREET.

BRIGHTON:
CELLARS,
30 KING'S ROAD.

BONDED STORES, CRESCENT VAULT, LONDON DOCKS, E.

Registered Telegraphic Address: **HEDGES BUTLER.**
Telephone No. 3809.

FOR WINES AND SPIRITS IN BOND SEE SPECIAL EXPORT LIST.

THE NINETEENTH CENTURY.

No. CI.—July 1885.

THE KHEDIVATE OF EGYPT.

For the last year or more to write upon Egypt at all has been an unwelcome task to those who have at heart the welfare of Egypt and the interests of England. The part of Cassandra is one for which I personally have never felt the slightest inclination or aptitude. When the Trojans had shown an invincible reluctance to admit the possibility of Troy being in danger from the Greeks, then, to my way of thinking, the daughter of Priam, if she had been well advised, would have kept silence even from good words. It would be absurd on my part to claim for my writings on the subject of Egypt the character of a warning such as that to which the discredited foreteller of Ilion's fate has for all time affixed her name. I wish it were equally absurd to suppose that the danger with which England is threatened by her culpable disregard of her interests in Egypt belonged to a similar category to that which brought about the ruin and fall of Troy. But in one respect I have long felt myself to bear a faint resemblance, at however remote an interval, to Cassandra, in virtue of the fact that the advice I have tendered has been received with utter incredulity. For years past, in the pages of this Review and elsewhere, I have sought, in season and out of season, to impress the truth that the establishment of a British Protectorate over Egypt is the course demanded by the vital interests of our Empire. But of late I have lost heart. If the evidence of stern facts, if the spectacle of the reverses, disasters, and humiliations which have resulted from the obstinate refusal of England to assert her mastery in Egypt, did not suffice to convince the British public of the necessity for action, it was obvious to me that no written words could suffice to bring the conviction home. It has always been my effort to look facts in the face, whether welcome or otherwise; and, so looking, I could not fail to recognise the fact that, under Mr. Gladstone's Administration, there was no possibility of our Egyptian policy being directed in accordance with English interests. This being so, it was idle to argue against a foregone conclusion. To get rid of Mr. Gladstone or to lose Egypt were, and are, the only alternatives before us. Which alternative I should choose it is needless to say; which alternative the country will choose it is impossible to say: but until this choice is made it is mere waste of breath for the partisans of a British Protectorate over Egypt to preach to deaf ears.

For this reason I for one should prefer to keep silence in respect of Egypt. We stand on the threshold of a new era. With the defeat and resignation of Mr. Gladstone's Government we are about to witness a change of Ministry, and we may trust also a change of policy. As to the result I am not over-sanguine. Still it is some comfort to reflect that the cards are about to be shuffled again, and that, bad as may be the hand dealt out to us, it cannot possibly be worse than that we have had hitherto. But there is, as I deem, a special reason why those who are interested in the future of Egypt should make their views known at this moment on one particular aspect of the Egyptian question. Of late the agitation in favour of a change in the Khedivate has assumed unwonted proportions. Under these circumstances, those who hold with me that the interest, the honour, and the duty of England are involved in the maintenance of Tewfik Pasha upon the Vice-regal throne are bound to make known their views.

Six years have passed since the deposition of Ismail Pasha and the consequent elevation of his eldest son to the Khedivate. The most persistent maligners of Tewfik have never even insinuated that he intrigued to oust his father from the throne. He owed his accession to the Khedivate simply and solely to the fact that he was next in the succession, and that it suited the policy of France and England to depose Ismail, but not to alter the succession. At the time he was made Khedive a tacit, if not an explicit, compact was entered into, to the effect that, on the one hand, he should rule in accordance with the advice of the two Powers, who by the act of Ismail's deposition had assumed a protectorate over Egypt, and, on the other hand, that, subject to the fulfilment of the above condition, he should be maintained on the throne by the Powers who had placed him there. Tewfik's part of the compact has been most loyally fulfilled; the part of the protecting Powers has been observed in the letter rather than in the spirit. It is obvious that the circumstances under which Tewfik acceded to the throne had dealt a mortal blow to the authority of the Khedivate. Ismail Pasha, in common with the other successors of Mehemet Ali, had possessed absolute and uncontrolled authority over Egypt, and had been credited by his people with even greater authority than he actually possessed. Effendina, the name by which he was called, means lord and master in the sense in which lordship and mastery are understood in the East—a sense which we of the Western world can hardly realise. To the ordinary Egyptian apprehension the Khedive was the embodiment of absolute supreme power, and when it was found that the Effendina could be dismissed by the European Powers at their own will and pleasure, the prestige of his supremacy was gone for ever. Even if Tewfik had been a man of the same stamp as the founder of his dynasty, he could not have wielded one half of the authority of the weakest of his predecessors. This decline in the power of the Khedivate, consequent on the deposition of Ismail, is entirely independent of the character of the individual Khedive. In politics the old nursery rhyme is pre-eminently true, and when Humpty Dumpty has once had a great fall, not all the king's horses and all the king's men can set Humpty Dumpty up again. But in the present instance the attempt to set Humpty Dumpty up again was conducted in a way which augmented the certainty of failure. The arrangement concluded on the deposition of Ismail, for the establishment of the Anglo-French Control, was carefully devised so as to restrict the authority of the Khedive and confirm the authority of the Controllers. Even this arrangement was so worked in practice as to deprive the Khedive of the appearance of sovereignty still left to him. Sir Evelyn Baring and M. de Blignières, the original Controllers, were men fond of power and apt to assert their supremacy. In this desire they were countenanced by Riaz Pasha, the Prime Minister of the day, who, being himself a man of energy and ambition, was ready enough to allow the Controllers to play the part of the supreme administrators of the country, if in the work of administration he could be permitted to monopolise the functions which under a less vigorous Control would have devolved upon the Khedive. When Sir Evelyn Baring left Egypt for India, his successor, Sir Auckland Colvin, followed the lead of M. de Blignières, and during the whole of the period which intervened between the deposition of Ismail and the Arabi insurrection Tewfik was treated as a puppet, whose showmen did not think it worth their while to conceal the action of the wires by which his movements were directed. The effacement of the Khedivate under the Control was undoubtedly facilitated by the personal character of the Khedive. Tewfik Pasha had been brought up at home under the oppressive tutelage of his father. He had, when he came to the throne, no experience of public affairs, little acquaintance with foreign languages, no knowledge of the art of government. Being regarded as a puppet, and treated as a cipher, he had scant opportunity of learning how to rule.

But he set himself resolutely to work, and all who know him will bear witness to the remarkable development of his character and the progress of his attainments under circumstances which would have led most Oriental princes to devote themselves to a life of sloth and self-indulgence.

Still, I fully admit that, under the Anglo-French Protectorate, as under the British military occupation, Tewfik has acquiesced in the control of his foreign protectors and advisers. It is very easy to say that if he had been a strong man he would not have so acquiesced, but if he had not acquiesced, the Control and the Protectorate would have been alike impossible. Whoever else may complain of Tewfik's conduct, it does not lie in the power of either England or France to reproach him for not having displayed qualities which would have been incompatible with the policy they have thought fit to pursue. As a matter of fact, up to the period of the military mutiny, Tewfik fulfilled his share of his compact with perfect good faith and loyalty. Equal good faith was not exhibited on the other side. When the Egyptian army led by Arabi first mutinied against the Government, it was the plain duty of England and France to furnish Tewfik with the support required to enable him to suppress the mutiny in its inception. The dispatch of a few hundred troops to Alexandria in February 1881, or even a distinct declaration that in case of need such a force would be dispatched, would have sufficed to secure the authority of the Khedive, and would have caused the insurrection which ended in Tel-el-Kebir to perish still-born. But the jealousies of France and England precluded any joint action, and Lord Granville's abortive promise of support, which in common with other promises of Mr. Gladstone's Government was not followed up by action, destroyed the prestige of England for the time in Egypt, and thus deprived Tewfik of the only weapon with which he could have resisted the progress of the insurrection. It is commonly asserted that, if Tewfik had been such a man as Mehemet Ali, or even as Ismail, he could have crushed the mutiny in its early days by an act of personal vigour. I very much doubt the truth of the assertion. The reason why Arabi would under like circumstances—in common with every one of his soldiers—have cringed in the dust before Ismail if His Highness had ordered him to give up his sword and fall upon his knees would have been because he knew that Ismail had absolute power to have him sent to the White Nile, or strangled, or bastinadoed to death, at his good will and pleasure. But Arabi and his fellow-conspirators were perfectly well aware that Tewfik had no power to execute summary punishment upon them without the consent of the Controllers; and that out of deference to European ideas such consent would not be forthcoming. The plain truth is that in the early stages of the mutiny Tewfik had no course open to him except to temporise with the mutineers, and he temporised accordingly.

The same defence may be urged in behalf of Tewfik's conduct during the period which intervened between Arabi's accession to power and the burning of Alexandria, supposing always that a defence is needed. The fact that Mr. Wilfrid Blunt declares that Tewfik acted in complicity with the military party is in itself, in the absence of any proof to the contrary, a reason to my mind for thinking that Tewfik did nothing of the kind. No evidence has been adduced to justify the reckless charges brought against Tewfik by the partisans of the mutiny ; and it is utterly contrary to human nature that Tewfik should in heart have desired the success of an insurrection which, if successful, must have eventuated in his own deposition, and in all likelihood, in his own assassination. Still, admitting for the sake of argument that Tewfik used language at times towards Arabi different from that which he employed to Sir Edward Malet, and that he professed sympathy with the aims of the insurgents—things of which there is no proof as yet forthcoming—I fail to see what cause of complaint we have against him. Until the day when our men-of-war opened fire on Alexandria there was absolutely no certainty whether the British Government would make up their minds to intervene. Time after time during the critical six months which preceded the bombardment Tewfik applied for aid and assistance to England. To these applications he could obtain no positive answer beyond vague assurances of good will, which his past experience of the vacillation of our Government had taught him to distrust. I say, without hesitation, that up to the final moment the English officials in Egypt felt no confidence in the ultimate intervention of England, and that Tewfik knew perfectly well that this was so. During the whole of the period in question Tewfik was haunted, and justly haunted, by the apprehension that, if he broke entirely with Arabi, he would be thrown over by England. Under these circumstances small blame attaches to Tewfik if, to some extent, he ran with the hare and hunted with the hounds ; if, while professing loyalty to England in his utterances to the British authorities, he assured his Ministers that in his heart he sympathised with their aims and objects. I do not say he did so—I only say that if he did so, he did what nineteen European princes out of twenty, and what every Oriental prince without exception, would have done in his place.

It is only fair to add that in the closing days of the insurrection, when once it had been made clear that England would stand by him, Tewfik displayed great personal courage and a firmness of purpose for which, beforehand, he would hardly have been given credit. During the three days in which his life was in hourly danger from the insurgents he held his ground with energy and dignity; and when he finally made good his escape under the protection of British troops, he was more respected by his people than he had ever been before or has been since. The reason of this is that he was deemed to have power and authority on his side. It is commonly assumed in discussions about Egypt, by persons who have no knowledge of the country, that Tewfik must be hated by his countrymen because he was a party to the suppression of a popular insurrection, by the aid of foreign troops. The assumption is based upon the delusion that you can argue by analogy from the workings of the European mind as to how the Oriental mind will be affected. A ruler is respected in the East, not because he rules in accordance with the wishes and prepossessions of his subjects, but because he is thought to be strong, able to reward, and powerful to punish. It matters nothing where his strength comes from, so long as the strength is—or is believed to be—there. In the interval between the bombardment of Alexandria and the battle of Tel-el-Kebir, Tewfik was deemed by his people to be strong, and was in consequence respected. As soon as it became obvious that the English were resolved to maintain Tewfik upon the throne, and to fight against his enemies, it seemed manifest to the Oriental mind that Tewfik would be supported in his authority by the might of the British Empire, or, in other words, that he would have power at his command. Unfortunately, the Oriental intellect, astute as it may be, is not astute enough to understand the character of Mr. Gladstone's statesmanship. We had no sooner replaced Tewfik upon the throne, at immense cost and at a heavy risk, than we proceeded to deprive him of all authority in the eyes of his people. The amnesty allotted to Arabi and the leaders of the insurrection was fatal to the authority, not only of Tewfik, but of the Khedivate. A ruler who is not allowed to punish rebels who have mutinied against his throne and conspired against his life is from an Oriental point of view not a ruler at all. When our Government, rightly or wrongly, decided to let Arabi go free, they rendered impossible the idea on which they had set their hearts—of governing Egypt through an independent native ruler.

The suppression of the rebellion and the release of the rebels were followed by the establishment of our Provisional Protectorate, during which Egypt has in fact, though not in name, been administered by a British Resident, first in the person of Lord Dufferin, and afterwards in that of Sir Evelyn Baring. Throughout the whole of this period our Government have persisted in repudiating any responsibility for the administration of Egypt. The fiction that the Khedive is an independent sovereign has been maintained almost as an article of faith by our Ministers at home. But in Egypt, where this contention was too absurd to be treated seriously, no attempt has been made to keep up an idle pretence. Constitutional fictions are utterly unintelligible to the Eastern mind. There a man rules or obeys, is either master or servant. Between the two there is no middle path; and by a ruler Orientals understand a man who has power to reward his friends and punish his enemies. Tewfik, being, by the conditions of our Protectorate, deprived of either faculty, is not, and cannot be, regarded by his people as a ruler. Still, with tact and discretion, much might have been done to keep up the semblance of authority which Tewfik nominally enjoys as the reigning sovereign of Egypt. The difficulties of Sir Evelyn Baring's position, as the representative of a Government which never knew its own mind from day to day, and which was always ignoring the advice and repudiating the action of its own agents, have been so great and manifest, that I feel too much allowance can hardly be made for any mistakes he may have committed. Still, amongst his many good qualities, tact and discretion are not the most prominent, and by lack of these qualities the position of Tewfik has been rendered more difficult than it must of necessity have been. Time after time, resolutions of importance have been taken without the approval and without the knowledge of the Khedive. Orders have been issued of which he has learned for the first time by seeing them in the Gazette. Appointments have been given to men notoriously out of favour at the Vice-regal Court. His private wishes in minor matters have been disregarded; his advice has been set aside ; and his endeavours to take an active part in the administration of his country have been studiously discouraged. His rare attempts to advance the interests of his personal friends have invariably resulted in those interests being thwarted by the action of the British representatives.

In saying this I do not wish to impugn the conduct of our representatives in Egypt. They might indeed have shown more regard for the external authority of the Khedive without impairing in any way the authority of England in Egypt. Still, so long as Egypt remains under a Protectorate, the Khedive must necessarily be a puppet; and this is the hard fact which dominates the whole situation. There may be two kings at Brentford, but there cannot be two kings at Cairo ; and the real king, so long as there is a Protectorate, single, dual, or multiple, must be, not the Khedive, but the representatives of the protecting body.

Of late there has been a cry raised that the failure of our administration in Egypt is due to the personal weakness of the Khedive. It is only in accordance with human nature that Mr. Gladstone and his colleagues should seek to prove that their mishaps in Egypt are not the result of their own mismanagement, but of causes beyond their control. Bad workmen always complain of their tools; and Tewfik has been the tool through which Mr. Gladstone's Government have had to administer Egypt. It has become, therefore, the fashion in official quarters to say that things might have gone very differently in Egypt if Tewfik had been a very strong ruler with a marked individuality of his own. Things in this event might have gone differently ; they certainly would have not gone better. A strong ruler, as Orientals understand strength, would never have acquiesced

in the subordinate position to which a native ruler is necessarily
reduced by the existence of a foreign Protectorate; he would either
have openly resisted the authority of the representatives of the protecting Power, or he would have secretly intrigued against them.
In either case, the protecting Power would have found it necessary
in self-defence to depose the native ruler or to reduce him to
obedience. Now Tewfik has facilitated, instead of impeding, the
action of his protectors; he has thrown no difficulties in their way;
he has carried out their instructions loyally and faithfully. He has
done all, and more than all, that could reasonably be expected of a
prince in his position. To speak the plain truth, Tewfik is the ideal
Khedive of a protected Egypt. In his public capacity he has given
us little or no cause of complaint; in his private and personal
capacity he has been above reproach. I do not profess to say that his
service has been rendered out of abstract regard for England; though
I am convinced that, by disposition and turn of mind, he prefers the
English to any other European nation; just as his father preferred
the French. But he would, I admit fully, serve a Dual or a
Multiple Protectorate as loyally as he has served the English one.
If Egypt could ever be made a really independent and self-governing
country, then I could understand the demand that a ruler of stronger
and sterner mould should be substituted for the reigning Khedive.
But for the present such a supposition is utterly impracticable. For
years to come Egypt must be ruled from abroad, and as the agent of
a foreign Power, Tewfik is the best prince that could be found.

Moreover, even if Tewfik's positive claims were far less strong than
I take them to be, his negative claims would be irresistible. Of the
changes which Ismail Pasha introduced into Egypt, the one whose advantages are least open to dispute is the alteration in the succession.
The rule prevalent in almost all Mussulman countries, by which the
succession is collateral instead of hereditary, is fruitful of evil.
Under the harem system family ties can hardly be said to exist
between the different members of whom an Eastern household is
composed. Brothers, born of different mothers, have very little in
common; and, as a rule, the men whom an Oriental prince has the
least cause to trust are his blood relations. The heir to the throne is
in most cases a man who is of much the same age with its occupant, is
regarded with suspicion by the sovereign, and in turn distrusts the
good faith of the sovereign. Even in Western States the relations
between a reigning prince and his heirs are not often harmonious.
But in the majority of cases this natural antagonism is mitigated by
the ties of close kinship and common interest which exist between
father and son and between them only. In the East, where those
mitigating influences do not exist, the effect is disastrous. The sovereign is, in fact, only a tenant for life, whose estate is bound to go after
his death to a collateral relation, with whom, in most instances, he is

on bad terms. He has no care, therefore, for the well-being of the country he administers, and devotes his energies to extracting as much as possible from it during his tenancy. It is greatly to Ismail Pasha's credit that he realised the evils of the Mahometan law of succession, and endeavoured by altering it to establish a continuity of interest between the successive sovereigns of Egypt. It would be a thousand follies to upset the principle of direct descent of which Tewfik is the impersonation, and even if any more eligible candidate for the post of Khedive were available, I should on this ground alone deprecate most ˉstrongly any interference with Tewfik's right to the throne.

But, as a matter of fact, there is no such candidate in existence. If Tewfik were to die, there would have to be a Regency till his eldest son came of age, which event would not take place for seven or eight years. I have seen it proposed that Tewfik should be urged to abdicate, and that an English official, probably our Consul-General, should be appointed Regent during the minority. The objections to a Regency are obvious enough; and the proposal to make an Englishman Regent would create as much or more opposition abroad as would be excited by the open declaration of a permanent Protectorate. The Porte again has suggested that Tewfik should be deposed, and that some high Turkish official, utterly unconnected with the dynasty of Mehemet Ali, such as Mouktar Pasha, should be entrusted with the administration of the country. In other words, Egypt would be reconverted into a Turkish Pashalik, and to this proposal neither England nor Europe could possibly consent. Again the idea has been broached of replacing Tewfik by one of his brothers, probably Hassan or Hussein. But, apart from the objection to thus resorting to the old rule of succession, there is not the slightest reason to suppose that any of the Khedive's brothers possess greater force of character or higher authority than himself, while they are entirely wanting in the remarkable personal merits which distinguish Tewfik from the rest of his family. As to Prince Halim, it may truly be said that he has no adherents beyond himself and the holders of his bonds. The Halim candidature has recently been explained in this Review with as much ability as the case admits of. But when all is said that can be said, the explanation only amounts to this—that Prince Halim, in his own opinion, would make an excellent Khedive. The theory is unsupported by any evidence; and the known facts are against it. The only claim Halim can allege—namely, that as the youngest son of Mehemet Ali, and the eldest male of the family next to Ismail, he ought to have succeeded by right to the Vice-regal throne at the deposition of the latter—would, for the reasons I have stated, be a positive disqualification, even if his personal merits recommended him for the post. But Halim's personal merits rest only on his own assertion. He left behind him a very bad reputation in Egypt previous to his exile. He was regarded there as one of the poorest specimens of the Turkish Pasha class. At Constantinople he has done nothing during his long residence to show that he has learnt experience by the troubles to which his own extravagance and mismanagement gave rise. For years he has been engaged in prosecuting a claim against the Egyptian Treasury, to which, in the opinion of independent judges, he has no title either in law or equity; and, unless public report belies him, he has repeatedly proposed to sacrifice the interests and the independence of Egypt, if by so doing he could induce the Porte to support his candidature for the Khedivate.

There remains one only possible substitute for Tewfik as Khedive; and the claims of this candidate are of a very different order to those of the others to whom I have alluded. I refer to the ex-Khedive. Upon this subject I would far sooner say nothing, if I thought it right to keep silence. It has been my fortune to see much of Ismail Pasha both on the throne and in exile; and—in common, for that matter, with all who have the pleasure of his acquaintance—I feel a difficulty in reconciling my feeling about His Highness with my judgment. It is impossible to know him without being impressed with his remarkable ability, without being influenced by his charm of manner, and without being biassed in his favour by the *bonhomie* he displayed in the days of his grandeur, and the dignity he has exhibited in the days of his adversity. To England, or at any rate to Englishmen, he has always been a friend; and if it were a question of his personal well-being alone, I should be loth to say a word against his return to Egypt, or even against his restoration to the throne. But when I see it seriously proposed that England should replace Ismail as Khedive, I have no choice except to speak out. It is now eight years ago since in the pages of this Review I was enabled to give the true story of the causes which had led Ismail Pasha into his embarrassments, and which had brought ruin upon the country over which he ruled. Long and intimate acquaintance with Egypt of a later date has fully confirmed me in the conviction that the story I then told erred, if it erred at all, in understating the case against His Highness. I fully admit that in judging of Ismail as a man you must make great allowances. Few rulers have ever been exposed to such temptations, have been surrounded by such evil advisers, or have been led astray to such an extent by their merits as well as by their failings. But in judging Ismail as a ruler you can make no such allowance. After all, it was his lavish extravagance, his greed of power, his hunger for appropriating to his own use the soil and the trade of Egypt, his love of intrigue and his passion for display which impoverished his country, destroyed the happiness and well-being of his people, and brought his dynasty to the verge of extinction. I may be told that Ismail has repented of his misdoings and seen the error of his ways. My answer is that, in public as in private life, the French proverb holds good, 'Qui a bu boira.' Give Ismail back his old power, and he will do with it again what he did before. The evidences of his having undergone a complete change of character are too slight to justify England in subjecting Egypt once more to the misery which he entailed upon her and upon her people. Nobody has written more strongly than I have done concerning the evils which our English policy, or want of policy, has entailed on Egypt. Still it is just never to lose sight of the fact that the deposition of Ismail and the rule of Tewfik as a protected prince, subject to British supervision, have very materially improved the condition of the fellaheen. The subject is too wide a one to enter on here. Let me only quote one passage from Sir Evelyn Baring's report of last January on the general situation of Egypt :—

When once the financial situation is regulated, all serious difficulties in connection with the government of Egypt proper will, I am convinced, disappear.

Everything else is going on very fairly well. I have before me at this moment a Report from Mr. Willcocks, who is one of Colonel Moncrieff's subordinates. 'From communications,' he says, 'with village sheikhs, fellaheen, and agents of non-resident landholders, it is evident that the kharadji tax of 30s. per acre does not press at all heavily on the vast majority of the people. There may be some whose lands have deteriorated, and who, in consequence, find it hard to pay, but such I have not found. On the contrary, the sheikhs and fellaheen declare that they are not only paying their taxes easily, but that they are paying off the debts contracted in Ismail Pasha's time, when 3*l*. or 4*l*. per acre were extracted from them.

'If six or seven more years of the just collection of taxes which has characterised Tewfik Pasha's reign are continued, they hope to be free of almost the whole of their burdens.'

To restore Ismail, if it means anything at all, means the restoration of the state of things under which the fellaheen were taxed to the uttermost limit of their resources, and ground down with debt.

My objection, however, to the restoration of Ismail is not based principally on the misery it might involve in its train. The strongest argument against the step in question is that, while it might do harm, it could not possibly do good. So long as we or any other European Power maintain our control over Egypt there is no room for a strong Khedive. An enormous deal of nonsense is talked about the personal authority of Ismail Pasha, and about the ease with which he would restore order to Egypt, supposing him to be ever replaced on the throne. Now, in as far as my experience goes, there is no country in the world where the personal authority of the ruler counts for so little as it does in Egypt. In the old days Ismail was all powerful in Egypt because his word was law; because he had power to punish those who displeased him, and to reward those who earned his favour. In one form or another, kourbash and backsheesh are the only two instruments of government in Egypt. Deprive a ruler of these instruments, and his power is gone, let his personal authority be what it may. What renders Tewfik's rule feeble is not that he is weak himself, but that he is powerless to punish his enemies or reward his friends. Put Ismail in Tewfik's position, subject to the same restrictions, and he will be as powerless as his son, and as unable to command obedience. Yet, so long as the English Protectorate endures, these restrictions must remain in force. We cannot allow a prince ruling under our protection, be he Tewfik, or Halim, or Ismail, to rule as an Oriental autocrat with the lives and liberties and fortunes of his subjects placed at his absolute disposal. Yet, unless he has this uncontrolled authority, the autocrat ceases to be feared, and can exert no influence which the protecting Power does not already possess.

There is one contingency, and one contingency alone, under which Ismail's return might be possible. If England should make up her mind to abandon Egypt, the control of the country would, whether we like it or not, pass into the hands of a European Commission in which the influence of France would be paramount. Now such a Commission, being influenced, as they would be, mainly by financial considerations, would be anxious to have as little to do as possible with the internal administration of the country. They would be very much in the position of an absentee landlord of a West Indian estate: where the overseer was given to understand that, so long as the rents were duly remitted, and so long as order was maintained on the plantation, no questions would be asked as to the means by which the revenue of the estate was secured, the mode in which things were kept quiet, or the extent to which he filled his own pockets. This is the sort of understanding that might, and probably would, be arrived at between the reigning Khedive and the International Commission by which Egypt is to be governed in the future if our Government will only consent to quit the country; and for carrying out such an arrangement Ismail possesses recommendations which Tewfik certainly does not. The influences, therefore, which are working in behalf of Ismail's restoration are identical with those which are working against English ascendency in Egypt, and in favour of placing the country under an International Syndicate. Any number of pleas are put forward to obscure the truth, but the plain fact is that the men who talk about the necessity of restoring Ismail do so because they wish to oust England out of Egypt and to restore the reign of kourbash and backsheesh in its integrity. If they do not mean this, it is because, like certain recent English apologists of Ismail, they do not understand the brief they have been instructed to hold, or do not know the facts of the case they have got to argue.

Meanwhile the duty of England seems to me clear. Tewfik has behaved loyally towards us, and we are pledged to his support by every consideration of interest and duty. If England is to maintain a general supervision over the administration of Egypt, she can find no Khedive better fitted to follow her instructions than Tewfik Pasha.

His fortunes are identified with ours, and whenever England leaves Egypt his fall is imminent; not from the fact that he is unpopular with his countrymen, but from the fact that he is viewed with disfavour by foreign Powers as being the nominee of England. His sons are being brought up under English teachers and educated at English schools, and until they at any rate have reached the age to reign, no arrangement could work more satisfactorily for England and for Egypt than the continuance of the present Khedivate.

Since the above lines were written, a Conservative Government has come into power. For reasons into which the limits of space preclude my entering, Egypt is almost the only field on which the new Government can give proof of their power of constructive statesmanship during the few months on which they can alone rely with certainty for their continuance in office. Between now and the general election it would be possible to make arrangements concerning Egypt which would secure the restoration of order and prosperity under a provisional Protectorate, in which England would play the part of the protecting power. By so doing a Conservative Ministry might do much to influence popular feeling in their favour, by showing that the interests of the Empire were safer under their own statesmanship than under that of the Liberals. Even if they failed to attain a majority at the coming election, they would leave behind them an achievement whose repute would stand them in good stead in the days to come. The opportunity is there if they only elect to seize it. But in order for any British Government, whether Conservative or Liberal, to be able to settle the Egyptian difficulty, it is essential they should look to facts, not to theories. Now the first of the facts connected with Egypt is that, if there is to be a Protectorate, the ruler must be a Khedive who will accept the position of a protected prince; and for this purpose Tewfik Pasha is eminently qualified, both by his merits and demerits, his failings and his virtues.

EDWARD DICEY

THE WORK OF VICTOR HUGO.

In the spring of 1616 the greatest Englishman of all time passed away with no public homage or notice, and the first tributes paid to his memory were prefixed to the miserably garbled and inaccurate edition of his works which was issued seven years later by a brace of players under patronage of a brace of peers. In the spring of 1885 the greatest Frenchman of all time has passed away amid such universal anguish and passion of regret as never before accompanied the death of the greatest among poets. The contrast is of course not wholly due to the incalculable progress of humanity during the two hundred and sixty-nine years which divide the date of our mourning from the date of Shakespeare's death : nor even to the vast superiority of Frenchmen to Englishmen in the quality of generous, just, and reasonable gratitude for the very highest of all benefits that man can confer on mankind. For the greatest poet of this century has been more than such a force of indirect and gradual beneficence as every great writer must needs be. His spiritual service has been in its inmost essence, in its highest development, the service of a healer and a comforter, the work of a redeemer and a prophet. Above all other apostles who have brought us each the glad tidings of his peculiar gospel, the free gifts of his special inspiration, has this one deserved to be called by the most beautiful and tender of all human titles—the son of consolation. His burning wrath and scorn unquenchable were fed with light and heat from the inexhaustible dayspring of his love —a fountain of everlasting and unconsuming fire. We know of no such great poet so good, of no such good man so great in genius : not though Milton and Shelley, our greatest lyric singer and our single epic poet, remain with us for signs and examples of devotion as heroic and self-sacrifice as pure. And therefore it is but simply reasonable that not those alone should mourn for him who have been reared and nurtured on the fruits of his creative spirit : that those also whom he wrought and fought for, but who know him only as their champion and their friend—they that cannot even read him, but remember how he laboured in their cause, that their children might fare otherwise than they—should bear no unequal part in the burden of this infinite and worldwide sorrow.

For us, who from childhood upwards have fostered and fortified whatever of good was born in us—all capacity of spiritual work, all seed of human sympathy, all powers of hope and faith, all passions and aspirations found loyal to the service of duty and of love—with the bread of his deathless word and the wine of his immortal song, the one thing possible to do in this first hour of bitterness and stupefaction at the sense of a loss not possible yet to realize, is not to declaim his praise or parade our lamentation in modulated effects or efforts of panegyric or of dirge: it is to reckon up once more the standing account of our all but incalculable debt. A brief and simple summary of his published works may probably lay before the student some points and some details not generally familiar to the run of English readers: and I know not what better service might be done them than to bring into their sight such aspects of the most multiform and many-sided genius that ever wrought in prose or verse as are least obvious and least notorious to the foreign world of letters.

Poet, dramatist, novelist, historian, philosopher, and patriot, the spiritual sovereign of the nineteenth century was before all things and above all things a poet. Throughout all the various and ambitious attempts of his marvellous boyhood—criticism, drama, satire, elegy, epigram, and romance—the dominant vein is poetic. His example will stand for ever as the crowning disproof of the doubtless more than plausible opinion that the most amazing precocity of power is a sign of ensuing impotence and premature decay. There was never a more brilliant boy than Victor Hugo: but there has never been a greater man. At any other than a time of mourning it might be neither unseasonable nor unprofitable to observe that the boy's early verse, moulded on the models of the eighteenth century, is an arsenal of satire on revolutionary principles or notions which might suffice to furnish forth with more than their natural equipment of epigram a whole army of reactionary rhymesters and pamphleteers. But from the first, without knowing it, he was on the road to Damascus: if not to be struck down by sudden miracle, yet by no less inevitable a process to undergo a no less unquestionable conversion. At sixteen he wrote for a wager in the space of a fortnight the chivalrous and heroic story of *Bug-Jargal*; afterwards recast and reinformed with fresh vigour of vitality, when the author had attained the maturer age of twenty-three. His tenderness and manliness of spirit were here made nobly manifest: his originality and ardour of imagination, wild as yet and crude and violent, found vent two years later in *Han d'Islande*. But no boyish work on record ever shewed more singular force of hand, more brilliant variety of power: though the author's criticism ten years later admits that 'il n'y a dans *Han d'Islande* qu'une chose sentie, l'amour du jeune homme; qu'une chose observée, l'amour de la jeune fille.' But as the work of a boy's fancy or invention, touched here and there with genuine humour, terror, and pathos, it is not less wonderful than are the author's first odes for ease and force and freshness and fluency of verse imbued with simple and sincere feeling, with cordial and candid faith. And in both these boyish stories the hand of a soldier's son, a child of the camp, reared in the lap of war and cradled in traditions of daring, is evident whenever an episode of martial adventure comes in among the more fantastic excursions of adolescent inventiveness. But it is in the ballads written between his twenty-second and his twenty-seventh year that Victor Hugo first showed himself, beyond all question and above all cavil, an original and a great poet. *La Chasse du Burgrave* and *Le Pas d'Armes du Roi Jean* would suffice of themselves to establish that. The fire, the music, the force, the tenderness, the spirit of these glorious little poems must needs, one would think, impress even such readers as might be impervious to the charm of their exquisitely vigorous and dexterous execution. It will of course, I should hope, be understood once for all that when I venture to select for special mention any special poem of Hugo's I do not dream of venturing to suggest that others are not or may not be fully as worthy of homage, or that anything of this incomparable master's work will not requite our study or does not demand our admiration ; I do but take leave to indicate in passing some of those which have been to me especially fruitful of enduring delight, and still are cherished in consequence with a peculiar gratitude.

At twenty-five the already celebrated lyric poet published his magnificent historic drama of *Cromwell* : a work sufficient of itself to establish the author's fame for all ages in which poetry and thought, passion and humour, subtle truth of character, stately perfection of structure, facile force of dialogue and splendid eloquence of style, continue to be admired and enjoyed. That the author has apparently confounded one earl of Rochester with another more famous bearer of the same title must not be allowed to interfere with the credit due to him for wide and various research. Any dullard can point the finger at a slip here and there in the history, a change or an error of detail or of date : it needs more care to appreciate the painstaking and ardent industry which has collected and fused together a great mass of historic and legendary material, the fervent energy of inspiration which has given life, order, and harmony to the vast and versatile design. As to the executive part of the poem, the least that can be said by any competent judge of that matter is that Molière was already equalled and Corneille was already excelled in their respective provinces of verse by the young conqueror whose rule was equal and imperial over every realm of song. The comic interludes or episodes of the second and third acts, so admirably welded into the structure or woven into the thread of the action, would suffice to prove this when collated with the seventeenth scene of the third act and the great speech of Cromwell in the fifth. The subtlety and variety of power displayed in the treatment of the chief character should be evident alike to those who look only on the upright side of it and those who can see only its more oblique aspect. The Cromwell of Hugo is as far from the faultless monster of Carlyle's creation and adoration as from the all but unredeemed villain of royalist and Hibernian tradition : he is a great and terrible poetic figure, imbued throughout with active life and harmonized throughout by imaginative intuition : a patriot and a tyrant, a dissembler and a believer, a practical humourist and a national hero.

The famous preface in which the batteries of pseudo-classic tradition were stormed and shattered at a charge has itself long since become a classic. That the greatest poet was also the greatest prose-writer of his generation there could no longer be any doubt among men of any intelligence : but not even yet was more than half the greatness of his multitudinous force revealed. Two years later, at the age of twenty-seven, he published the superb and entrancing *Orientales*: the most musical and many-coloured volume of verse that ever had glorified the language. From *Le Feu du Ciel* to *Sara la Baigneuse*, from the thunder-peals of exterminating judgment to the flute-notes of innocent girlish luxury in the sense of loveliness and life, the inexhaustible range of his triumph expands and culminates and extends. Shelley has left us no more exquisite and miraculous piece of lyrical craftsmanship than *Les Djinns*; none perhaps so rich in variety of modulation, so perfect in rise and growth and relapse and reiterance of music. And here, like Shelley, was Hugo already the poet of freedom, a champion of the sacred right and the holy duty of resistance. The husk of a royalist education, the crust of reactionary misconceptions, had already begun to drop off : not yet a pure republican, he was now ripe to receive and to understand the doctrine of human right, the conception of the common weal, as distinguished from imaginary duties and opposed to hereditary claims.

The twenty-eighth year of his life, which was illuminated by the issue of these passionate and radiant poems, witnessed also the opening of his generous and lifelong campaign or crusade against the principle of capital punishment. With all possible reverence and all possible reluctance, but remembering that without perfect straightforwardness and absolute sincerity I should be even unworthier than I am to speak of Victor Hugo at all, I must say that his reasoning on this subject seems to me insufficient and inconclusive : that his own radical principle, the absolute inviolability of human life, the absolute sinfulness of retributive bloodshedding, if not utterly illogical and untenable, is tenable or logical only on the ground assumed by those quaintest though not least pathetic among fanatics and heroes, the early disciples of George Fox. If a man tells you that supernatural revelation has forbidden him to take another man's life under all and any circumstances, he is above or beyond refutation : if he says that self-defence is justifiable, and that righteous warfare is a patriotic duty, but that to exact from the very worst of murderers, a parricide or a poisoner, a Philip the Second or a Napoleon the Third, the payment of a life for a life—or even of one infamous existence for whole hecatombs of innocent lives—is an offence against civilisation and a sin against humanity, I am not merely unable to accept but incompetent to understand his argument. We may most heartily agree with him that France is degraded by the guillotine, and that England is disgraced by the gallows, and yet our abhorrence of these barbarous and nauseous brutalities may not preclude us from feeling that a dealer (for example) in professional infanticide by starvation might very properly be subjected to vivisection without anæsthetics, and that all manly and womanly minds not distorted or distracted by prepossessions or assumptions might rationally and laudably rejoice in the prospect of this legal and equitable process. 'The senseless old law of retaliation' (*la vieille et inepte loi du talion*) is inept or senseless only when the application of it is false to the principle: when justice in theory becomes unjust in practice. Another stale old principle or proverb—'abusus non tollit usum'—suffices to confute some of the arguments—I am very far from saying, all—adduced or alleged by the ardent eloquence of Victor Hugo in his admirable masterpiece of terrible and pathetic invention, *Le dernier jour d'un condamné*, and subsequently in the impressive little history of *Claude Gueux*, in the famous speech on behalf of Charles Hugo when impeached on a charge of insult to the laws in an article on the punishment of death, and in the fervent eloquence of his appeal on the case of a criminal executed in Guernsey, and of his protest addressed to Lord Palmerston against the horrible result of its rejection. That certain surviving methods of execution are execrable scandals to the country which maintains them, he has proved beyond all humane or reasonable question: and that all murderers are not alike inexcusable is no less indisputable a proposition: but beyond these two points the most earnest and exuberant advocacy can advance nothing likely to convince any but those already converted to the principle that human life must never be taken in punishment of crime—that there are not criminals whose existence insults humanity, and cries aloud on justice for mercy's very sake to cut it off.

The next year (1830) is famous for ever beyond all others in the history of French literature: it was the year of *Hernani*, the date of liberation and transfiguration for the tragic stage of France. The battle which raged round the first acted play of Hugo's and the triumph which crowned the struggles of its champions, are not these things written in too many chronicles to be for the thousandth time related here? And of its dramatic and poetic quality what praise could be uttered that must not before this have been repeated at least some myriads of times? But if there be any mortal to whom the heroic scene of the portraits, the majestic and august monologue of Charles the Fifth at the tomb of Charles the Great, the terrible beauty, the vivid pathos, the bitter sweetness of the close, convey no sense of genius and utter no message of delight, we can only say that it would simply be natural, consistent, and proper for such a critic to recognize in Shakespeare a barbarian, and a Philistine in Milton.

Nevertheless, if we are to obey the perhaps rather childish impulse of preference and selection among the highest works of the highest among poets, I will avow that to my personal instinct or apprehension *Marion de Lorme* seems a yet more perfect and pathetic masterpiece than even *Hernani* itself. The always generous and loyal Dumas placed it at the very head of his friend's dramatic works. Written, as most readers (I presume) will remember, before its predecessor on the stage, it was prohibited on the insanely fatuous pretext that the presentation of King Louis the Thirteenth was an indirect affront to the majesty of King Charles the Tenth. After that luckless dotard had been driven off his throne, it was at once proposed to produce the hitherto interdicted play before an audience yet palpitating with the thrill of revolution and resentment. But the chivalrous loyalty of Victor Hugo refused to accept a facile and factitious triumph at the expense of an exiled old man, over the ruins of a shattered old cause. The play was not permitted by its author to enter till the spring of the following year on its inevitable course of glory. It is a curious and memorable fact that the most tenderhearted of all great poets had originally made the hero of this tragedy leave the heroine unforgiven for the momentary and reluctant relapse into shame by which she had endeavoured to repurchase his forfeited life; and that Prosper Mérimée should have been the first, Marie Dorval the second, to reclaim a little mercy for the penitent. It is to their pleading that we owe the sublime pathos of the final parting between Marion and Didier.

In one point it seems to me that this immortal masterpiece may perhaps be reasonably placed, with *Le Roi s'amuse* and *Ruy Blas*, in triune supremacy at the head of Victor Hugo's plays. The wide range of poetic abilities, the harmonious variety of congregated powers, displayed in these three great tragedies through almost infinite variations of terror and pity and humour and sublime surprise, will seem to some readers, whose reverence is no less grateful for other gifts of the same great hand, unequalled at least till the advent in his eighty-first year of *Torquemada*.

Victor Hugo was not yet thirty when all these triumphs lay behind him. In the twenty-ninth year of a life which would seem fabulous and incredible in the record of its achievements if divided by lapse of time from all possible proof of its possibility by the attestation of dates and facts, he published in February *Notre-Dame de Paris*, in November *Les Feuilles d'Automne*: that the two dreariest months of the year might not only 'smell April and May,' but outshine July and August. The greatest of all tragic romances has a Grecian perfection of structure, with a Gothic intensity of pathos. To attempt the praise of such a work would be only less idle than to refuse it. Terror and pity, with eternal fate for keynote to the strain of story, never struck deeper to men's hearts through more faultless evolution of combining circumstance on the tragic stage of Athens. Louis the Eleventh has been painted by many famous hands, but Hugo's presentation of him, as compared for example with Scott's, is as a portrait by Velasquez to a portrait by Vandyke. The style was a new revelation of the supreme capacities of human speech: the touch of it on any subject of description or of passion is as the touch of the sun for penetrating irradiation and vivid evocation of life.

From the *Autumn Leaves* to the *Songs of the Twilight*, and again from the *Inner Voices* to the *Sunbeams and Shadows*, the continuous jet of lyric song through a space of ten fertile years was so rich in serene and various beauty that the one thing notable in a flying review of its radiant course is the general equality of loveliness in form and colour, which is relieved and heightened at intervals by some especial example of a beauty more profound or more sublime. The first volume of the four, if I mistake not, won a more immediate and universal homage than the rest: its unsurpassed melody was so often the raiment of emotion which struck home to all hearts a sense of domestic tenderness too pure and sweet and simple for perfect expression by any less absolute and omnipotent lord of style, that it is no wonder if in many minds—many mothers' minds especially—there should at once have sprung up an all but ineradicable conviction that no subsequent verse must be allowed to equal or excel the volume which contained such flowerlike jewels of song as the nineteenth and twentieth of these unwithering and imperishable *Leaves*. But no error possible to a rational creature could be more serious or more complete than the assumption of any inferiority in the volume containing the two glorious poems addressed to Admiral Canaris, the friend (may I be forgiven the filial vanity or egotism which impels me to record it?) of the present writer's father in his youth; the two first in date of Hugo's finest satires, the lines that scourge a backbiter and the lines that brand a traitor (the resonant and radiant indignation of the latter stands unsurpassed in the very *Châtiments* themselves); the two most enchanting aubades or songs of sunrise that ever had outsung the birds and outsweetened the flowers of the dawn; and—for here I can cite no more—the closing tribute of lines more bright than the lilies whose name they bear, offered by a husband's love at the sweet still shrine of motherhood and wifehood. And in each of the two succeeding volumes there is, among all their other things of price, a lyric which may even yet be ranked with the highest subsequent work of its author for purity of perfection, for height and fulness of note, for music and movement and informing spirit of life. We ought to have in English, but I fear—or rather I am only too sure—we have not, a song in which the sound of the sea is rendered as in that translation of the trumpet-blast of the night-wind, with all its wails and pauses and fluctuations and returns, done for once into human speech and interpreted into spiritual sense for ever. For instinctive mastery of its means and absolute attainment of its end, for majesty of living music and fidelity of sensitive imagination, there is no lyric poem in any language more wonderful or more delightful. A yet sweeter and sadder and more magical sea-song there was yet to come years after—but only from the lips of an exile. Of the ballad—so to call it, if any term of definition may suffice—which stands out as a crowning splendour among *Les Rayons et les Ombres*, not even Hugo's own eloquence, had it been the work (which is impossible) of any other great poet in all time, could have said anything adequate at all. Not even Coleridge and Shelley, the sole twin sovereigns of English lyric poetry, could have produced this little piece of lyric work by combination and by fusion of their gifts. The pathetic truthfulness and the simple manfulness of the mountain shepherd's distraction and devotion might have been given in ruder phrase and tentative rendering by the nameless ballad-makers of the border: but here is a poem which unites something of the charm of *Clerk Saunders* and *The Wife of Usher's Well* with something of the magic of *Christabel* and the *Ode to the West Wind*: a thing, no doubt, impossible; but none the less obviously accomplished.[1]

The lyric work of these years would have been enough for the energy of another man, for the glory of another poet; it was but a

---

[1] In the winter of the year which in spring had seen *Les Rayons et les Ombres* come forth to kindle and refresh the hearts of readers, Victor Hugo published an ode in the same key as those *To the Column* and *To the Arch of Triumph*, on the return and reinterment of the dead Napoleon. Full of noble feeling and sonorous eloquence, the place of this poem in any collection of its author's works is distinctly and unmistakably marked out by every quality it has and by every quality it wants. In style and in sentiment, in opinion and in rhythm, it is one with the national and political poems which had already been published by the author since the date of his *Orientales*: in other words, it is in every possible point utterly and absolutely unlike the poems long afterwards to be written by the author in exile. Its old place, therefore, in all former editions, at the end of the volume containing the poems previously published in the same year, is obviously the only right one, and rationally the only one possible. By what inexplicable and inconceivable caprice it has been promoted to a place, in the so-called *édition définitive*, on the mighty roll of the *Légende des Siècles*, at the head of the fourth volume of that crowning work of modern times, I am hopelessly and helplessly at a loss to conjecture. But, at all risk of impeachment on a charge of unbecoming presumption, I must and do here enter my most earnest and strenuous protest against the claim of an edition to be in any sense final and unalterable, which rejects from among the *Châtiments* the poem on the death of Saint-Arnaud and admits into the *Légende des Siècles* the poem on the reinterment of Napoleon.

part, it was (I had well-nigh said) the lesser part, of its author's labours—if labour be not an improper term for the successive or simultaneous expressions or effusions of his indefatigable spirit. The year after *Notre-Dame de Paris* and *Les Feuilles d'Automne* appeared one of the great crowning tragedies of all time, *Le Roi s'amuse*. As the key-note of *Marion de Lorme* had been redemption by expiation, so the key-note of this play is expiation by retribution. The simplicity, originality, and straightforwardness of the terrible means through which this austere conception is worked out would give moral and dramatic value to a work less rich in the tenderest and sublimest poetry, less imbued with the purest fire of pathetic passion. After the magnificent pleading of the Marquis de Nangis in the preceding play, it must have seemed impossible that the poet should without a touch of repetition or reiterance be able again to confront a young king with an old servant, pour forth again the denunciation and appeal of a breaking heart, clothe again the haughtiness of honour, the loyalty of grief, the sanctity of indignation, in words that shine like lightning and verses that thunder like the sea. But the veteran interceding for a nephew's life is a less tragic figure than he who comes to ask account for a daughter's honour. Hugo never merely repeats himself: his miraculous fertility and force of utterance were not more indefatigable and inexhaustible than the fountains of thought and emotion which fed that eloquence with fire.

Marion de Lorme had been prohibited by Charles the Tenth for an imaginary reflection on Charles the Tenth; *Le Roi s'amuse* was prohibited by Louis-Philippe the First—and Last—for an imaginary reflection on Citizen Philippe Égalité. Victor Hugo vindicated his meaning and reclaimed his rights in a most eloquent, most manly, and most unanswerable speech before a tribunal which durst not and could not but refuse him justice. Early in the following year he brought out the first of his three tragedies in prose—in a prose which even the most loyal lovers of poetry, Théophile Gautier at their head, acknowledged on trial to be as good as verse. And assuredly it would be, if any prose ever could : which yet I must confess that I for one can never really feel to be possible. *Lucrèce Borgia*, the first-born of these three, is also the most perfect in structure as well as the most sublime in subject. The plots of all three are equally pure inventions of tragic fancy: Gennaro and Fabiano, the heroic son of the Borgia and the caitiff lover of the Tudor, are of course as utterly unknown to history as is the self-devotion of the actress Tisbe. It is more important to remark and more useful to remember that the mastery of terror and pity, the command of all passions and all powers that may subserve the purpose of tragedy, is equally triumphant and infallible in them all. *Lucrèce Borgia* and *Marie Tudor* appeared respectively in February and in November of the year 1833: *Angelo*, two years later; and the year after this the exquisite and melodious libretto of

La Esmeralda, which should be carefully and lovingly studied by all who would appreciate the all but superhuman versatility and dexterity of metrical accomplishment which would have sufficed to make a lesser poet famous among his peers for ever, but may almost escape notice in the splendour of Victor Hugo's other and sublimer qualities. In his thirty-seventh year all these blazed out once more together in the tragedy sometimes apparently rated as his master-work by judges whose verdict would on any such question be worthy at least of all considerate respect. No one that I know of has ever been absurd enough to make identity in tone of thought or feeling, in quality of spirit or of style, the ground for a comparison of Hugo with Shakespeare: they are of course as widely different as are their respective countries and their respective times: but never since the death of Shakespeare had there been so perfect and harmonious a fusion of the highest comedy with the deepest tragedy as in the five many-voiced and many-coloured acts of *Ruy Blas*.

At the age of forty Victor Hugo gave to the stage which for thirteen years had been glorified by his genius the last work he was ever to write for it. There may perhaps be other readers besides myself who take even more delight in *Les Burgraves* than in some of the preceding plays which had been more regular in action, more plausible in story, less open to the magnificent reproach of being too good for the stage—as the *Hamlet* which came finally from the recasting hand of Shakespeare was found to be, in the judgment even of Shakespeare's fellows; too rich in lyric beauty, too superb in epic state. The previous year had seen the publication of the marvellously eloquent, copious, and vivid letters which gave to the world the impressions received by its greatest poet in a tour on the Rhine made five years earlier—that is, in the year of *Ruy Blas*. In this book, as Gautier at once observed, the inspiration of *Les Burgraves* is evidently and easily traceable. Among numberless masterpieces of description, from which I have barely time to select for mention the view of Bishop Hatto's tower by the appropriately Dantesque light of a furnace at midnight—not as better than others, but as an example of the magic by which the writer imbues and impregnates observation and recollection with feeling and with fancy—the most enchanting legend of enchantment ever written for children of all ages, and sweet and strange enough to have grown up among the fairy tales of the past whose only known authors are the winds and suns of their various climates, lurks like a flower in a crevice of a crumbling fortress. The entrancing and haunting beauty of Régina's words as she watches the departing swallows—words which it may seem that any one might have said, but to which none other could have given the accent and the effect that Hugo has thrown into the simple sound of them—was as surely derived, we cannot but think, from some such milder and brighter vision of the remembered Rhineland solitudes, as were the sublime and all but Æschylean imprecations of Guanhumara from the impression of their darker and more savage memories or landscapes.

Two years before the appearance of *Les Burgraves* Victor Hugo had begun his long and glorious career as an orator by a speech of characteristically generous enthusiasm, delivered on his reception into the Academy. The forgotten playwright and versifier whom he succeeded had been a professional if not a personal enemy: the one memorable thing about the man was his high-minded opposition to the tyranny of Napoleon, his own personal friend before the epoch of that tyranny began: and this was the point at once seized and dwelt on by the orator in a tone of earnest and cordial respect. The fiery and rapturous eloquence with which at the same time he celebrated the martial triumphs of the empire gave ample proof that he was now, as his father had prophesied that his mother's royalist boy would become when he grew to be a man, a convert to the views of that father, a distinguished though ill-requited soldier of the empire, and a faithful champion or mourner of its cause. The stage of Napoleonic hero-worship, single-minded and single-eyed if short-sighted and misdirected, through which Victor Hugo was still passing on towards the unseen prospect of a better faith, had been vividly illustrated and vehemently proclaimed in his letters on the Rhine, and was hereafter to be described with a fervent and pathetic fidelity in a famous chapter of *Les Misérables*. The same phase of patriotic prepossession inspired his no less generous tribute to the not very radiant memory of Casimir Delavigne, to whom he paid likewise the last and crowning honour of a funeral oration: an honour afterwards conferred on Frédéric Soulié, and far more deservedly bestowed on Honoré de Balzac. More generous his first political speech in the chamber of peers could not be, but there was more of reason and justice in its fruitless appeal for more than barren sympathy, for a moral though not material intervention, on behalf of Poland in 1846. His second speech as a peer is an edifying commentary on the vulgar English view of his character as defective in all the practical and rational qualities of a politician, a statesman, or a patriot. The subject was the consolidation and defence of the French coast-line: a poet, of course, according to all reasonable tradition, if he ventured to open his unserviceable lips at all on such a grave matter of public business, ought to have remembered what was expected of him by the sagacity of blockheads, and carefully confined himself to the clouds, leaving facts to take care of themselves and proofs to hang floating in the air, while his vague and verbose declamation wandered at its own sweet will about and about the matter in hand, and never. came close enough to grapple it. This, I regret to say, is exactly what the greatest poet of his age was inconsiderate enough to avoid, and most markedly to abstain from doing; a course of conduct which can only be attributed to his notorious and deplorable love of paradox. His speech, though not wanting in eloquence of a reserved and masculine order, was wholly occupied with sedate and business-like exposition of facts and suggestion of remedies, grounded on experience and study of the question, and resulting in a proposal at once scientific and direct for such research as might result if possible in an arrest of the double danger with which the coast was threatened by the advance of the Atlantic and the Channel, to a gradual obstruction of the great harbours, and by the withdrawal or subsidence of the Mediterranean from the sea-ports of the south; finally, the orator urged upon his audience as a crowning necessity the creation of fresh harbours of refuge in dangerous and neglected parts of the coast; insisting, with a simple and serious energy somewhat unlike the imaginary tone of the typical or traditional poet, on the homely fact that ninety-two ships had been lost on the same part of the coast within a space of seven years, which might have been saved by the existence of a harbour of refuge. To an Olympian or a Nephelococcygian intelligence such a paltry matter should have been even more indifferent than the claim of a family of exiles on the compassion of the country which had expelled them. To my own more humble and homely understanding it seems that there are not many more significant or memorable facts on record in the history of our age than this: that Victor Hugo was the advocate whose pleading brought back to France the banished race of which the future representative was for upwards of twenty years to keep him in banishment from France. On the evening of the same day on which the house of peers had listened to his speech in behalf of the Bonaparte family, Louis-Philippe, having taken cognizance of it, expressed his intention to authorize the return of the brood whose chief was hereafter to pick the pockets of his children. In the first fortnight of the following year the future author of the terrible *Vision of Dante* saluted in words full of noble and fervent reverence the apostle of Italian resurrection and Italian unity in the radiant figure of Pope Pius the Ninth. When the next month's revolution had flung Louis-Philippe from his throne, Victor Hugo declined to offer himself to the electors as a candidate for a seat in the assembly about to undertake the charge of framing a constitution for the commonwealth: but if summoned by his fellow-citizens to take his share of this task, he expressed himself ready to discharge the duty so imposed on him with the disinterested self-devotion of which his whole future career was to give such continuous and such austere evidence. From the day on which sixty thousand voices summoned him to redeem this pledge, he never stinted nor slackened his efforts to fulfil the charge he had accepted in the closing words of a short, simple, and earnest address, in which he placed before his electors the contrasted likenesses of two different republics; one, misnamed a commonweal, the rule of the red flag, of barbarism and blindness, communism and proscription and revenge: the other a commonweal indeed, in which all rights should be respected and no duties evaded or ignored; a government of justice and mercy, of practicable principles and equitable freedom, of no iniquitous traditions and no utopian aims. To establish this kind of commonwealth and prevent the resurrection of the other, Hugo, at the age of forty-six, professed himself ready to devote his life. The work of thirty-seven years is now before all men's eyes for proof how well this promise has been kept. On dangerous questions of perverse or perverted socialism (June 20, 1848), on the freedom of the press, on the state of siege, its temporary necessity and its imminent abuse, on the encouragement of letters and the freedom of the stage, he spoke, in the course of a few months, with what seems to my poor understanding the most admirable good sense and temperance, the most perfect moderation and loyalty. I venture to dwell upon this division of Hugo's life and labours with as little wish of converting as I could have hope to convert that large majority whose verdict has established as a law of nature the fact or the doctrine that 'every poet is a fool' when he meddles with practical politics; but not without a confidence grounded on no superficial study that the maintainers of this opinion, if they wish to cite in support of it the evidence supplied by Victor Hugo's political career, will do well to persevere in the course which I will do them the justice to admit that—as far as I know—they have always hitherto adopted; in other words, to assume the universal assent of all persons worth mentioning to the accuracy of this previous assumption, and dismiss with a quiet smile or an open sneer the impossible notion that any one but some single imbecile or eccentric can pretend to take seriously what seems to them ridiculous, or to think that ridiculous which to their wiser minds commends itself as serious. This beaten road of assumption, this well-worn highway of assertion, is a safe as well as a simple line of travel: and the practical person who keeps to it can well afford to dispense with argument as palpably superfluous, and with evidence as obviously impertinent. Should he so far forget that great principle of precaution as to diverge from it into the humble and homely course of investigation and comparison of theory with fact and probability with proof, his task may be somewhat harder, and its result somewhat less than satisfactory. I would not advise any but an honest and candid believer in the theory which identifies genius with idiocy—which at all events would practically define one special form of genius as a note of general idiocy—to study the speeches (they are nine in number, including two brief and final replies to the personal attacks of one Montalembert, whose name used to be rather popular among a certain class of English journalists as that of a practical worshipper of their great god Compromise, and a professional enemy of all tyranny or villany that was not serviceable and obsequious to his Church)—to study, I say, the speeches delivered by Victor Hugo in the Legislative Assembly during a space of exactly two years and eight days. The first of these speeches dealt with the question of what in England we call pauperism—with the possibility, the necessity, and the duty of its immediate relief and its ultimate removal : the second, with the infamous and inexpiable crime which diverted against the Roman republic an expedition sent out under the plea of protecting Rome against the atrocities of Austrian triumph. A double-faced and double-dealing law, which under the name or the mask of free education aimed at securing for clerical instruction a monopoly of public support and national encouragement, was exposed and denounced by Hugo in a speech which insisted no less earnestly and eloquently on the spiritual duty and the spiritual necessity of faith and hope than on the practical necessity and duty of vigilant resistance to priestly pretention, and vigilant exposure of ecclesiastical hypocrisy and reactionary intrigue. Against 'the dry guillotine' of imprisonment in a tropical climate added to transportation for political offences, the whole eloquence of a heart as great as his genius was poured forth in fervour of indignation and pity, of passion and reason combined. The next trick of the infamous game played by the conspirators against the commonwealth, who were now beginning to show their hand, was the mutilation of the suffrage. To this again Victor Hugo opposed the same steadfast front of earnest and rational resistance ; and yet again to the sidelong attack of the same political gang on the existing freedom of the press. A year and eight days elapsed before the delivery of his next and last great speech in the Assembly which he would fain have saved from the shame and ruin then hard at hand—the harvest of its own unprincipled infatuation. The fruit of conspiracy, long manured with fraud and falsehood and all the furtive impurities of intrigue, was now ripe even to rottenness, and ready to fall into the hands already stretched towards it—into the lips yet open to protest that no one— the accuser himself must know it—that no one was dreaming of a second French empire. All that reason and indignation, eloquence and argument, loyalty and sincerity could do to save the commonwealth from destruction and the country from disgrace, was done : how utterly in vain is matter of history—of one among the darkest pages in the roll of its criminal records. The voice of truth and honour was roared and hooted down by the faction whose tactics would have discredited a den of less dishonest and more bare-faced thieves ; the stroke of state was ready for striking ; and the orator's next address was the utterance of an exile.

There are not, even in the whole work of Victor Hugo, many pages of deeper and more pathetic interest than those which explain to us 'what exile is.' Each of the three prefaces to the three volumes of his *Actes et Paroles* is rich in living eloquence, in splendid

epigram and description, narrative and satire and study of men and
things: but the second, it seems to me, would still be first in attraction, if it had no other claim than this, that it contains the record of
the death of Captain Harvey. No reverence for innocent and heroic
suffering, no abhorrence of triumphant and execrable crime, can
impede or interfere with our sense of the incalculable profit, the
measureless addition to his glory and our gain, resulting from Victor
Hugo's exile of nineteen years and nine months. Greater already
than all other poets of his time together, these years were to make
him greater than any but the very greatest of all time. His first task
was of course the discharge of a direct and practical duty; the record
or registration of the events he had just witnessed, the infliction on
the principal agent in them of the simple and immediate chastisement consisting in the delineation of his character and the recapitulation of his work. There would seem to be among modern
Englishmen an impression—somewhat singular, it appears to me, in
a race which professes to hold in special reverence a book so dependent
for its arguments and its effects on a continuous appeal to conscience
and emotion as the Bible—that the presence of passion, be it never
so righteous, so rational, so inevitable by any one not ignoble or
insane, implies the absence of reason; that such indignation as
inflamed the lips of Elijah with prophecy, and armed the hand of
Jesus with a scourge, is a sign—except of course in Palestine of old—
that the person affected by this kind of moral excitement must needs
be a lunatic of the sentimental if not rather of the criminal type.
The main facts recorded in the pages of *Napoléon le Petit* and
L'Histoire d'un Crime are simple, flagrant, palpable, indisputable.
The man who takes any other view of them than is expressed in these
two books must be prepared to impugn and to confute the principle
that perjury, robbery, and murder are crimes. But, we are told, the
perpetual vehemence of incessant imprecation, the stormy insistence
of unremitting obloquy, which accompanies every chapter, illuminates
every page, underlines every sentence of the narrative, must needs
impair the confidence of an impartial reader in the trustworthiness
of a chronicle and a commentary written throughout as in characters
of flaming fire. Englishmen are proud to prefer a more temperate,
a more practical, a more sedate form of political or controversial
eloquence. When I remember and consider certain examples of
popular oratory and controversy now flagrant and flourishing among
us, I am tempted to doubt the exact accuracy of this undoubtedly
plausible proposition: but be that as it may, I must take leave to
doubt yet more emphatically the implied conclusion that the best
or the only good witness procurable on a question of right and wrong
is one too impartial to feel enthusiasm or indignation; that indifference alike to good and evil is the sign of perfect equity and trustworthiness in a judge of moral or political questions; that a man

who has witnessed a deliberate massacre of unarmed men, women, and children, if he be indiscreet enough to describe his experience in any tone but that of scientific or æsthetic serenity, forfeits the inherent right of a reasonable and an honourable man to command a respectful and attentive hearing from all honourable and reasonable men.

But, valuable and precious as all such readers will always hold these two books of immediate and implacable history, they will not, I presume, be rated among the more important labours of their author's literary life. No one who would know fully or would estimate aright the greatest genius born into the world in our nineteenth century can afford to pass them by with less than careful and sympathetic study: for without moral sympathy no care will enable a student to form any but a trivial and a frivolous judgment on writings which make their primary appeal to the conscience—to the moral instinct and the moral intelligence of the reader. They may perhaps not improperly be classed, for historic or biographic interest, with the *Littérature et Philosophie mêlées* which had been given to the world in 1834. From the crudest impressions of the boy to the ripest convictions of the man, one common quality informs and harmonizes every stage of thought, every phase of feeling, every change of spiritual outlook, which has left its mark on the writings of which that collection is composed; the quality of a pure, a perfect, an intense and burning sincerity. Apart from this personal interest which informs them all, two at least are indispensable to any serious and thorough study of Hugo's work: the fervent and reiterated intercession on behalf of the worse than neglected treasures of mediæval architecture then delivered over for a prey to the claws of the destroyer and the paws of the restorer; the superb essay on Mirabeau, which remains as a landmark or a tidemark in the history of his opinions and the development of his powers. But the highest expression of these was not to be given in prose—not even in the prose of Victor Hugo.

ALGERNON CHARLES SWINBURNE.

(*To be concluded.*)

MODERN CATHOLICS AND SCIENTIFIC FREEDOM.

A LOVE for the contemplation of living nature has existed amongst the most civilised nations in all ages, and amongst many nations which no one would call civilised. The prehistoric representations of the reindeer and the mammoth seem to speak to us of the existence of such a sentiment in very early times, and what is regarded as the oldest of our sacred books is replete with evidences of careful observations of birds and beasts, as well as with references to phenomena of inanimate nature. The names of Aristotle, Albertus Magnus, and Humboldt stand out as representing an encyclopædic knowledge of and love for nature in classical, mediæval, and modern times. Nevertheless, such a love for nature, however delightful to those who felt it, and however indirectly influential on the welfare of populations and the general progress of men socially, could not be said to exercise any direct, plainly visible influence on the social and political condition of the world. It is otherwise now. Biology, the science which treats of living organisms—the natural history, that is, of animals and plants—a science which was once little more than an affair of taste, has now become a power, and its direct bearing on the happiness of human life is generally recognised. It is possible that in a cell of some remote Carthusian monastery which has hitherto escaped the destroying hand of revolution there may yet linger an aged monk who dreams that the study of animals and plants is still but an amusement for the 'ingenious,' over and above some practical utility it may have for the practitioner of medicine. But no man who has any real acquaintance with the world and its ways can now be ignorant that biology has passed from the laboratories of men of science, through the boudoirs of fashion, to the cabinets of Ministers and to popular platforms, there to exercise a direct influence on the government of States and the prosperity of Churches, an influence which the progress of democracy is likely to accelerate and to augment.

That this is no exaggerated statement of the facts is witnessed for by the words of men whose positions and antecedents afford a sufficient guarantee that they are not likely to overstate the claims of physical science or to favour its prospects unduly to the detriment of anterior agencies and organisations.

Thus the Rev. Dr. Barry, a distinguished Catholic writer and former Professor of Divinity, has published [1] the following noteworthy statements: 'It is an undeniable fact that a priesthood of physical science now exists and has superseded, or is threatening to supersede, all other priesthoods; ... and the multitude ... is now feeling, not vaguely, but with a fast-growing consciousness, that the last word rests neither with priests nor philosophers, but with the profession of physics, or, as it is loosely termed, with science.' If such is indeed the case—and my own experience strongly confirms the Rev. Dr. Barry's affirmation—then it is plainly high time that any clergy which would retain its influence should not only understand somewhat of biology, but be able to point to some recognised experts in that science amongst its members. Dr. Barry recognises this need, and says [2] that the clergy would not have come to occupy the less influential position they now do, had not Christian teachers betrayed their trust. 'We are now,' he continues, 'in no small measure reaping the reward of our disdain of the " things that are made," to which St. Paul directed his gaze and that of his disciples when he would demonstrate the invisible things of God.' He also forcibly points out that 'a high authority in Rome, Father Palmieri, has remarked, with as much truth as point, in his *Institutes of Philosophy*, that one of the greatest calamities of the last three centuries has been the neglect of the study of physical science by orthodox Christians.'

But a voice which Catholics must regard as of all but the highest authority has recently issued from Rome, recommending to the clergy in no hesitating or doubtful terms the cultivation of science. That estimable and learned Benedictine, Cardinal Pitra, has published [3] an eloquent letter in the same sense. Therein he says:—

> It is good that the clergy, who have in their theology the key to all sciences, should neglect none of them, and we ought also to have our specialists. ... It is important that, with a rich store of the science of the sanctuary, the clergy should not be strangers to that other knowledge of which the world is proud. ... There is in these studies, which are dry at first sight, pure and healthy delight, which grows towards enthusiasm in the measure in which one cultivates with perseverance the at first thorny field. It is well that the young clergy should consecrate their leisure and spare energy to these labours.

What makes this letter of even more value than its own intrinsic merit, is the obvious reflection that it would not have been published without the tacit approval of the learned Pontiff now ruling over the Catholic Church—a Pontiff who himself uttered the following memorable words in favour of the most scrupulous truthfulness and painstaking accuracy in the pursuit of historical science :—

---

[1] In a very admirable article entitled 'The Battle of Theism,' which appeared in the *Dublin Review* for October 1884, p. 274. This article well deserves perusal by men of science, no less than by theologians.

[2] *Loc. cit.* pp. 275–287.

[3] In the April number of a new series of a periodical called *Cosmos*.

It is hard to conceive how much harm may be done by a study of history devoted to party ends. . . . For it becomes not the guide of life, nor the light of truth, but the accomplice of vices and the agent of destruction. . . . Men are needed who will set themselves to write with the intention and aim of making known the truth in all fulness and strength. . . . The first law of history is to dread uttering falsehood; the next is not to fear stating the truth; lastly, that the historian's writings should be open to no suspicion of partiality or of animosity.—*Letter of Leo XIII.*, dated the 18th of August 1883.

The aim of the first contributions which I had the honour to make to this Review—that is, to the Review which, with another title, was publ'shed under the same editorial care—was to show the compatibility which I believed, and believe, to exist between the most advanced science and the most orthodox Christianity. As a faithful student of that science which from my earliest years has had an insuperable attraction for me, I have ever been careful to abate no jot or tittle of the just claims of Biology. As a loyal son of the Catholic Church I have been no less careful not to put forward one statement in the interests of conciliation which had not received the sanction of well-known and universally esteemed experts in theology. Having thus ventured to assume the responsible position of such a peacemaker upon certain very definite grounds, I should feel bound in honour and honesty to withdraw my apology and confess myself to have been mistaken if through new scientific discoveries, or fresh dogmatic decisions, those grounds ceased in my opinion to be capable of sustaining my argument. No man can be either truly scientific or truly religious who does not set truth pure and simple above every other consideration, whatever it may be.

Now since the publication of the article above referred to, certain more or less authoritative statements have been made in a sense hostile to my own views, which seem to demand some notice at my hands, as, if they were well founded and if the Catholic Church were really committed to such statements, then I should, however unintentionally, have been guilty of misleading readers who had accepted my statements as valid.

A very remarkable article[4] by the Rev. Jeremiah Murphy has been recently published in an ecclesiastical periodical, which, I am told, is regarded as having much weight and importance. Therein that gentleman does me the honour to criticise my views as to evolution in general, and as to the evolution of man's body in particular. I have to thank him for the courteous way in which he expresses himself in my regard, but he none the less condemns most uncompromisingly all those points the possibility if not the probability of which I especially desired to establish. Thus he altogether denies that Catholics are free to hold the doctrine that the

---

[4] Entitled 'Evolution and Faith.' It appeared in the *Irish Ecclesiastical Record* for December 1884, pp. 756-767.

body of the first man was naturally evolved by the same ordinary secondary laws which have (in the judgment of everyone competent to offer an opinion on the subject) evolved the bodies of his fellow-animals.

He tells us that [5]

in testing the orthodoxy of this theory there is, happily, no need to discuss orchids and troglodytes, or the various families of the Lemuridæ. . . . We can apply to it the unerring rule, 'quod semper, ubique, &c.'; and if, tested by this rule, Mr. Mivart's theory be found wanting, then his scientific speculations must be unsound. . . . We may not be able to point to a solemn definition . . . but this is by no means necessary. For if the immediate formation of the bodies of our first parents be asserted by the voice of the *ordinary magisterium* of the Church, then are we as strictly bound to believe it as if it had been defined by a General Council, or by a Pope teaching *ex cathedra.*

He then refers to the constitution 'Dei Filius' of the Vatican Council, to Pius the Ninth's letter to the Archbishop of Munich, and to the twenty-second proposition of the Syllabus, and continues:

Now the theologians and teachers of the Catholic Church assert with the most extraordinary unanimity the *immediate formation* of the bodies of our first parents, and such unanimous teaching is, according to the Vatican Council and Pius the Ninth, obligatory upon us, and consequently we are not free to hold the evolution theory even with reference to the body of the first man.

So direct, so precise, so circumstantial is the Scriptural account of man's creation, that, if the evolution theory were true, the sacred writers, if they intended to deceive us, could not have chosen language better calculated to effect that end: 'And the Lord God *formed* man out of the slime of the earth' (Genesis). 'Thy hands have made me and fashioned me' (Job). Now the ordinary meaning of such texts (and they are very numerous) is unquestionably the *immediate formation* by God of the bodies of Adam and Eve. And on this ordinary meaning we can insist, unless the evolutionists show that there is sufficient reason for departing from it. *This they have not done*; and consequently the *prima facie* Scriptural view of man's creation need not be abandoned.[6]

Mr. Murphy cites a variety of theologians, ancient and modern, against me. Amongst them, one named 'Punch,' a distinguished Irish theologian; also Perrone, Ubaldi, Mazzella, Lamy, and Jungman of Louvain, the two latter being said to 'hold that the application of the evolution theory even to plants and animals mentioned in Genesis is incompatible with the true meaning of the text.'

He further says:—

Are we then to abandon the faith of all past ages for the dreamings of a few would-be philosophers of the present day who are blinded by excessive light? Are we to bend and strain Revelation to suit the speculations of even well-meaning men? The Catholic Church welcomes every fresh accession of knowledge; she blesses and honours the votaries and promoters of real science; but she reminds them, in the language of Pius the Ninth,[7] that in their search for knowledge Revelation must be

---

[5] 'Evolution and Faith,' pp. 760, 761, and 765–767.

[6] Surely because a thing *need* not be abandoned,' it does not follow that others should be *forbidden* to abandon it.

[7] In his 1863 letter to the Archbishop of Munich.

their guiding star. The Church has seen many enemies, has witnessed many revolutions, has braved many storms; and wherever science, falsely so-called, clashes with her deposit of faith, she greets it with bold defiant front. She does not tolerate it, nor does she fear it. And from the issue of such conflicts in the past we can well infer what shall be the issue of any such in the future. When many of the biological speculations of our time will have gone down into the grave in which Gnosticism lies mouldering, forgotten, the Church of God will be what she has ever been since her foundation, the sole faithful, fearless witness, teacher, and guardian of all revealed truth. That some of the advocates of evolution mean well to the Church is quite certain; but the adoption of this theory by Catholics is 'a new fashion of an old sin.' It is an instance of a tendency that is becoming too common—that of minimising Catholic doctrine; of diluting it, so as to suit the tactics of a class of persons from whom the Church has nothing to expect and nothing to fear.[8]

My own statements he expressly and emphatically contradicts, saying:[9] 'Now in the face of this consensus of Catholic teaching, what becomes of the boasted 'orthodoxy' of the evolution theory? What becomes of the assertion, 'that the strictest Ultramontane Catholics are perfectly free to hold the doctrine of evolution'? referring to words of mine which were first addressed to the readers of this Review.[10] Thus addressed, I feel that as an honest man anxious not even passively to minister to untruth, I have no choice but to accept Mr. Murphy's challenge, and, after carefully weighing his words and my own, to publicly retract or reaffirm my position according to the value I believe due to his denunciations.

For his denunciations have a very formidable sound, and the words of the various authorities referred to by him would have to be respectfully considered seriatim, were it not for a certain 'previous question.'

As the matter stands, however, I have not even the smallest intention of considering them, of disputing the aptness of Mr. Murphy's quotations, or questioning his accuracy as to the meanings he assigns to the authorities on whom he relies. Neither will I seek to controvert the justness of his deductions from the principles he lays down, and still less will I retract what I have advanced. I will do none of these things, because I think that his premises and principles are demonstrably false, and that his judgments, therefore, need be of no concern whatever to those persons who in addition to scientific knowledge possess some acquaintance with the history of the seventeenth century. I will do my best to show that such is the case, not only because I feel I owe such a demonstration to any persons who may have been influenced by my former publications, but also because, if unrefuted, Mr. Murphy may obtain the, by him certainly, most undesired success of persuading some lovers of nature

---

[8] As if the prospect of either might be an adequate motive for modifying a doctrine irrespective of its truth or falsehood!
[9] *Loc. cit.* p. 765.
[10] Though he refers to them as given in my *Lessons from Nature*, p. 430.

that there is an incompatibility between biological science and Christian dogma, and that Church membership, therefore, is no longer a possibility for them. But, in fact, the position assumed by Mr. Murphy is one only too familiar to us, and familiarity with it has not bred esteem for it. He has, indeed, but ranged himself amongst the ever-recurring band of obstructives who always turn out to have been in the wrong : amongst such as in the first age of the Church upheld the belief in a speedy end to the world ; who afterwards denied the existence of antipodes ; who, later, opposed the liberalism of St. Thomas Aquinas and the other advocates of Aristotle ; who subsequently declared that to affirm the earth's motion and the sun's stability was heresy ; and who denounced as usurers the individuals who timidly began to develop the great modern system of finance and commercial credit. Such objections as his were brought forward again and again to oppose the promulgators of all the truths or economical improvements which such narrow-minded obstructives decried or impeded.

And here some of those persons who were ever opposed to such apologies as mine may not unreasonably exclaim, ' And these ecclesiastical obstructives have spoken with an authority which all true and consistent Catholics are bound to respect, and therefore there is after all a radical and insuperable antagonism between science and the Church !' At the risk, however, of being thought to deal in paradox, I reply that, as circumstances have turned out, it is the very distinctness and authority with which scientific truths have been condemned which make secure, beyond all possibility of question, the complete scientific freedom of sincere Catholics who are logical and will not shut their eyes to God's teaching through the history of His Church. That such is the case I will shortly endeavour to make plain. Before doing so, however, I would say a few words to those who may feel impatient at being called upon to consider such a question at all, and who think that it can be a matter of no consequence to them, or to the progress of the world, what Catholics may or may not hold to be incumbent on their acceptance and belief. I would ask such persons to bear in mind how large is the number of most estimable men and women who still bow down their consciences before that great ecclesiastical tribunal whose President rules from the Vatican, and to reflect that it must be a gain to science, and therefore to the welfare and progress of mankind, if such men and women can be made aware that the most scrupulous loyalty to their religion is perfectly compatible with the freest speculation and most untrammelled advance in every field of science without exception.

For science tends to suffer from a mistake as to this matter. I know a priest now living (much esteemed, and who often teaches from a London pulpit) who lately avowed his belief that the sun and the whole sidereal heavens do actually revolve round the earth every twenty-four hours; adding that he believed this because he considered that the Church was committed to that view by its decision with respect to Galileo. I also knew another very excellent priest, for a time the head of a college, who exclaimed to me, 'How glorious it would be if it should turn out after all that the sun did move round the earth, and that the Church had therefore been all this time in the right about the matter!' The influence of such convictions not only on the minds of those who possess them, but also on those subject to their authority, must tend to produce a distaste for physical science, and must every now and then divert some probably fruitful mind from following scientific pursuits; while, on the other hand, the influence of such priests as Father Secchi, Father Perry, F.R.S., Father David, Father Hahn, Father Klein, F.L.S., the Rev. Dr. Barry, the Rev. Robert F. Clarke, F.L.S., the Rev. Gordon Thompson, and many more that I could name, would tend to promote a love for physical science, and to direct towards that field of ever-fruitful labour, minds which but for such influence might have been directed to commercial pursuits.

Thus not only religion, but science, would have suffered if the conviction of their scientific freedom was not felt by Catholics. For eminent biologists, at the same time sincere Catholic laymen, were till lately, or are still, living amongst us, such as John Müller, Schwan (the originator of the great 'cell' theory), J. Andrew Wagner, Delpino, Van Beneden, and Gaudry. There are also to my knowledge Catholics, both laymen and ecclesiastics, whose names are not generally known, but who are devoted to the pursuit not only of physical but of biological science. It seems, therefore, plainly to the advantage of science in the future, as well as in the past, that no needless supposition opposed to the perfect intellectual freedom of Catholics should be permitted to subsist.

That such perfect intellectual freedom does exist can, I think, be unanswerably demonstrated by a careful consideration of the memorable conflict between science and ecclesiastical authority in the past. That conflict was in many respects similar to the contest which now exists between the teaching of the most competent biologists on the one hand, and that of such theologians as the Rev. Jeremiah Murphy and his allies, together with the cloud of witnesses and authorities he quotes, on the other.

For a most instructive parallelism exists between the opposition of our present ecclesiastical obstructives to evolution, and that offered by their predecessors to Copernicanism, although no authoritative declarations against evolution can be cited which are nearly so strong as those which could be brought forward against the views of Galileo by his opponents. I would refer my readers to a very remarkable and able work by the Rev. W. W. Roberts, which has just been published by Messrs. Parker and Co. Therein he points out the incompleteness and consequent error of the article on Galileo in that generally most excellent work, the *Catholic Dictionary*, and proves how utterly untenable are the views which were propounded and the position taken up by the late Dr. Ward, in the *Dublin Review*, with respect to Galileo. The following quotations are from the recently published work here referred to :—

In the year 1615, Cardinal Bellarmine, writing to Father Foscarini, the Carmelite, said :—

You are aware that the Council of Trent forbids us to interpret Scripture in a sense opposed to the consent of the Holy Fathers; and if your paternity will read, I do not say only the Holy Fathers, but also modern commentators on Genesis, the Psalms, Ecclesiastes, Josue, you will find that they all adhere to the literal exposition that the sun is in the heaven, and revolves round the earth with very great velocity, and that the earth is very far from the heaven, and remains immovable in the centre of the universe. Consider with yourself as a man of prudence whether the Church can permit Scripture to be interpreted in a sense opposed to the mind of the Holy Fathers and all modern commentators.

In 1616 the Sacred Congregation of the Index made, as everyone knows, a solemn decree about ' that false Pythagorean doctrine, altogether opposed to the divine Scripture, on the mobility of the earth and the immobility of the sun,' by which the works of Copernicus and others were placed on the Index. But there is much more of ecclesiastical authority than this against that Copernicanism which everyone now accepts as a demonstrated truth of science. By order of Pope Urban the Eighth, the Inquisition formally promulgated certain statements for the express purpose that Catholic men of science might be informed what they were to hold on this subject. These statements were as follows :—

That the sun is the centre of the universe and immovable from its place is absurd, philosophically false, and formally heretical, because it is expressly contrary to Holy Scripture.

That the earth is not the centre of the universe nor immovable, but that it moves and also has diurnal motion, is absurd, philosophically false, and, theologically considered, is at least erroneous in faith.

In the sentence pronounced on Galileo by the Inquisition we read :—

Invoking the most Holy Name of our Lord Jesus Christ and that of His most glorious mother Mary ever Virgin, by this our definitive sentence we say, pronounce, judge, and declare that you, the said Galileo, on account of the things proved against you by documentary evidence, and which have been confessed by you as aforesaid, have rendered yourself to this Holy Office vehemently suspected of heresy—that is, of having believed and held a doctrine which is false and contrary to the sacred and divine Scriptures—to wit, that the sun is in the centre of the world, and that it does not move from east to west, and that the earth moves and is not the centre of the universe ; *and that an opinion can be held and defended as probable after it has been declared and defined to be contrary to Holy Scripture.*

Galileo himself was compelled to say, ' With a sincere heart and faith unfeigned, I abjure, curse, and detest the above-named errors and heresies.'

Finally, Pope Alexander the Seventh, in 1664, by his bull, *Speculatores Domus Israel*, confirmed and approved the prohibitions contained in the former decrees of the Congregation of the Index, which had been published in 1616.[11]

Now it is just possible that some thoughtless objector may say that when authority declared Galileo's opinions to be contrary to Scripture and the unanimous consent of the Fathers, all that was meant was that they contradicted the *letter*, and not necessarily the *spirit* of Scripture and the Fathers. But it is as clear as daylight that no Papal or other authority was needed to declare that contradiction as regards the *letter*. That was conceded on both sides. It was Scripture regarded as the 'word of God' which was in question, otherwise how could contradicting it be *heresy* ? Galileo was suspected of holding the Copernican theory, and *therefore* of *heresy*. ' I am,' he was made to say, ' suspected of *heresy, that is*, that I hold that the earth moves and that the sun does not ; ' and, to make the matter quite clear in the ' monition,' it was expressly stated that Copernicus was suspended because his principles were contrary to Scripture and *its true and Catholic interpretation.*

Another objector may urge that the decision was on a matter outside those subjects as to which infallibility has been given to supreme ecclesiastical authority—outside, that is, the *depositum fidei*—and that it concerned a matter of science, not of ' faith and morals.' But this, again, may be replied to very shortly. For when a judge decides a point, he, *ipso facto*, decides that it is within his province to judge concerning it. What is or is not within the supreme authority's province to decide must be known to that authority. An infallible authority must know the limits of its revealed message. If authority can make a mistake in determining its own limits, it may make a mistake in a matter of faith.

Now, what is the upshot of these twin condemnations of the seventeenth and of the nineteenth centuries, and these parallel repudiations by ecclesiastical authorities of the teachings of science? What is their bearing on the duties of Catholic men of science generally—whether they be students of astronomy, geology, biology, history, or Biblical criticism? Significant, indeed, is that upshot, and most important that bearing.

I have often heard it exclaimed, ' How providential was that Divine influence which guarded the Pope from addressing to the universal Church any decree formally excommunicating all adherents of Copernicanism thenceforth for all time ! '

Viewing these events, however, in the light of our present knowledge, Catholics may far more thankfully exclaim : ' How providential

---

[11] This fact has been discovered and published for the first time by the Rev. W. W. Roberts. (See his work before referred to.)

was that Divine permission by which such ecclesiastical authorities were allowed to fall into such egregious errors!'

But what was the real nature of these errors? It has often been audaciously affirmed that Galileo was condemned for proposing an unorthodox interpretation of Scripture, and that authority made no judgment concerning physics, and took no action which impeded the development of science.

But the exact contrary to this is the very truth. Ecclesiastical authority *did* give a judgment directly affecting physics, and which impeded scientific progress. It went therefore *ultra vires*, but it did much more than that. It founded its erroneous decree affecting physical science, which was *not* its own province, upon an erroneous judgment about the meaning of Scripture,[12] which was universally supposed *to be* its own province. In this important matter it was the man of science that was right and ecclesiastical authority that was wrong. The latter sought to impose, and more or less succeeded in imposing, an erroneous belief as to God's word, from which erroneous belief science has delivered us. It is true that all opposition to Copernicanism has now ceased, but authority has not yet confessed and apologised for its mistaken action with respect to Galileo and Copernicus.[13] Catholics, however, have now much cause to be thankful for such acts, however much they may be inclined to reprobate them; for it is those very acts, seen in the light of subsequent history, which have relieved them at once and for ever from a burden which would, but for such relief, be intolerable.

The men of science were indeed contented with respectfully disregarding Scriptural expressions, seeing that some of them in their literal sense were as inconsistent with the physics of St. Thomas as with the physics of Galileo, and they therefore regarded such expressions as unimportant to religion. But it was ecclesiastics who would not be content with this, but who insisted that they were important to religion, and believed they were themselves divinely commissioned to declare their true meaning, which they therefore attempted to fix. By this course of action they have succeeded in demonstrating not only our freedom with respect to such passages of Scripture, but also, what they little deemed of, our freedom, as good Catholics, with respect to ecclesiastical decrees also. The moderation of Galileo and his good sense are indeed remarkable, considering the

---

[12] Strange to say, this pregnant fact was never called attention to before the publication of the Rev. W. W. Roberts's study of the question.

[13] The wrong that Copernicus suffered was not in his lifetime, the condemnation by Rome of his opinions being occasioned by the condemnation of those of his illustrious scientific successor. As to Galileo, both his right to make a will and of burial in consecrated ground were disputed, and Pope Urban interfered to prevent the erection of a monument to him (for which much money had been subscribed) in Santa Croce at Florence. His body was therefore buried in an obscure corner, and his monument was not erected till a century later.

era in which he lived. In his letter to Christina, the Grand Duchess of Tuscany, he says (I give Mr. Drinkwater's translation) :—

I am inclined to believe that the intention of the sacred Scriptures is to give mankind the information necessary for their salvation, and which, surpassing all human knowledge, can by no other means be accredited than by the mouth of the Holy Spirit. But I do not hold it necessary to believe that the same God who has endowed us with senses, with speech and intellect, intended that we should neglect the use of these, and seek by other means for knowledge which they are sufficient to procure us; especially in a science like astronomy, of which so little notice is taken in the Scriptures, that none of the planets except the Sun and Moon, and once or twice only Venus, under the name of Lucifer, are so much as named there. This, therefore, being granted, methinks that in the discussion of natural problems we ought not to begin at the authority of texts of Scripture, but at sensible and necessary demonstrations; for, from the Divine word the sacred Scripture and nature did both alike proceed, and I conceive that, concerning natural effects, that which either sensible experience sets before our eyes, or necessary demonstrations do prove unto us, ought not upon any account to be called into question, much less condemned, upon the testimony of Scriptural texts, which may under their words couch senses seemingly contrary thereto.

Again, to command the very professors of astronomy that they of themselves see to the confuting of their own observations and demonstrations is to enjoin a thing beyond all possibility of doing, for it is not only to command them not to see that which they do see, and not to understand that which they do understand, but it is to order them to seek for and to find the contrary of that which they happen to meet with. I would entreat these wise and prudent Fathers that they would with all diligence consider the difference that is between opinionative and demonstrative doctrines; to the end that, well weighing in their minds with what force necessary inferences urge us, they might the better assure themselves that it is not in the power of the professors of demonstrative sciences to change their opinions at pleasure, and adopt first one side and then another; and that there is great difference between commanding a mathematician or a philosopher and the disposing of a lawyer or a merchant; and that the demonstrated conclusions touching the things of nature and of the heavens cannot be changed with the same facility as the opinions are touching what is lawful or not in a contract, bargain, or bill of exchange. Therefore, first let these men apply themselves to examine the arguments of Copernicus and others, and leave the condemning of them as erroneous and heretical to whom it belongeth; yet let them not hope to find such rash and precipitous determinations in the wary and holy Fathers, or in the absolute wisdom of him who cannot err, as those into which they suffer themselves to be hurried by some particular affection or interest of their own. In these and such other positions, which are not directly articles of faith, certainly no man doubts but his Holiness hath always an absolute power of admitting or condemning them; but it is not in the power of any creature to make them to be true or false otherwise than of their own nature and in fact they are.

The proceedings which occurred with respect to Galileo afford us an actual demonstration of two most noteworthy facts. One is that what is declared by authoritative congregations to be at once against the teaching of Scripture, of the holy Fathers, and of antecedent ecclesiastical tribunals concerning a matter touching science, may none the less be true. The second noteworthy fact is, that men of science may have a truer perception of what Scripture must be held (since it is inspired) to teach, than may be granted to ecclesiastical authorities. This is demonstrated by the fact that those who held the very Catholic truth in the seventeenth century were not the inquisitors, but those whom they so rashly condemned.[14]

Pious Catholics have then great cause for thankfulness, for it has thus been made absolutely and unanswerably plain and clear to them by the voice of history (which they are bound to hold not merely with Schiller as the judgment of mankind but as the judgment of God) what are their duties in the pursuit of science. God has thus taught us that it is not to ecclesiastical congregations but to men of science that He has committed the elucidation of scientific questions, whether such questions are or are not treated of by Holy Scripture, by the writings of the Fathers and Doctors of the Church, and by ecclesiastical assemblages and tribunals. Moreover, the freedom thus so happily gained for astronomical science has, of course, been gained for all science—geology, biology, sociology, political economy, history, and Biblical criticism—for whatever, in fact, comes within the reach of human inductive research, and is capable of verification. This, moreover, necessarily includes the scientific criticism of those very Scriptures which ecclesiastical authority in the seventeenth century plainly showed its inability either scientifically or theologically to comprehend. Manifestly such questions as the authorship and the dates of the various sacred books, as well as of the temporal circumstances which their writers may show they were influenced by, with the general scope and intention of each respectively, cannot be withdrawn from scientific inquiry, when it must be admitted that men of science so succeeded and that ecclesiastical authority so failed in interpreting the true and inspired meaning of God's written word. Well may the modern Catholic, when considering the happy results to his freedom of the fault committed at Rome with respect to Galileo, borrow the words the Church uses on Holy Saturday with respect to Adam's fall, and exclaim with all his heart, *Oh, felix culpa!* Oh, happy fault which has brought us so great a redemption!

There is yet another aspect of this question about which Catholics have cause for deep thankfulness. Its ethical aspect shows us how much we have gained through the moral [15] no less than the scientific advance of modern times. As the authorities who condemned Galileo were ignorant not only of the physical knowledge of our day but of the physical knowledge of their own day—a better acquaintance with

---

[14] Our present illustrious Pontiff, Leo XIII., published a pastoral letter in February 1877 (the year before his elevation to the Papacy), in which he himself tells us that 'Galileo, who gave to experimental philosophy one of its most vigorous impulses, reached, *by means of his researches*, the *proof* that *Holy Scripture* and nature equally exhibit the footprints of the Deity.'

[15] Amongst the conspicuous and undeniable ethical advances which have been made by us, as compared with our fathers of the seventeenth and earlier centuries, are—(1) the recognition of the claims of the individual conscience to practical respect; (2) the perception of the moral guilt of gambling, as in State lotteries; and (3) the awakening to the fact that animals have rights, and that wanton cruelty is a sin.

which ought to have saved them from their blunder—as also they were ignorant of those economical truths which their successors now not only confess but make use of; so also they appear to have had no glimmering of perception of the practical claims of the most sacred and inalienable of all rights—the rights of conscience. They seem to have had no fear whatever lest by their threats of temporal disadvantage they should play the devil's part and tempt Galileo to make an oath against his conscience. Those who most sympathise with him can have little doubt but that in his abjuration he did perjure himself. Of that crime, however, the judges who tempted him to it must take their share. Nor should we, much as we blame Galileo's act, think too severely of the unhappy actor himself. Aged and infirm, he weakly erred through dread of the dire consequences which he, as a heretic, might otherwise incur. He surely calls far more for pity than for moral reprobation from us, who happily have no fear of being called to make so terrible a choice, and have no such fear just because it is the progress of ethical as well as of physical science which has made it impossible for us now to be tempted by terror of bodily suffering to err as did Galileo or as did Galileo's judges. The duty of acting according to conscience was indeed unhesitatingly laid down by mediæval theologians who have been quoted and their teaching nobly enforced by our illustrious fellow-countryman Cardinal Newman.[16] But the practical consequences [17] of such teaching have been effectively deduced only in modern times. It would now be generally recognised as a moral truism, that all the citizens of a State save one, would be morally culpable did they try and force that one to perform acts against his conscience such as might be to curse the Koran, to tread upon the Cross, or to salute the Host.

Thanks to our progress, it has now become plain to all men that no fear inspired by threats of fire, whether temporal or eternal, ought to make the man of science swerve for a hair's breadth from the duty he owes to God of declaring the very truth with respect to those laws which God has instituted.

Nevertheless, no candid men, whether Catholics or not, who are familiar with the history of the sixteenth and seventeenth centuries can doubt but that a sincere conviction of duty, however mistaken, animated the authorities both of the Inquisition and the Congregation of the Index. If our pity may be justly claimed for Galileo, it seems to be yet more called forth by the spectacle of venerable ecclesiastics, whose office constituted them the guardians of right against might, led by a mistaken estimate of the powers entrusted to them,

[16] In his letter to the Duke of Norfolk.
[17] That the term 'freedom of conscience' may be used in quite another sense from that in which we moderns generally use it, is proved by the language sometimes employed by the late Dr. Ward. In a controversy about 'liberty of conscience,' he actually once ventured to go so far as to affirm that 'a Catholic's freedom of conscience is grievously impaired by the civil tolerance of other religions' (*Dublin Review*, January 1876, vol. xxvii. p. 14).

not only to impede the progress of science which some of them really desired to favour, but even to betray the cause of that very authority the supremacy of which it was their great object to secure.

Let me now return to the subject of evolution and theology with the light gained from the previous conflict respecting astronomy. That certain good Catholics who are devoted to science are distressed and more or less paralysed by such declarations as those of Mr. Murphy, I happen to know with certainty. To such I offer the foregoing observations, which I think will effectually dissipate their scruples. Men of science of the seventeenth century were appalled and paralysed by the condemnation of Galileo. Descartes, in his letter to Mersenne, declares how that event almost decided him to burn his papers, or at least to let no one see them, and he refrained from publishing his treatise on the World. Catholic men of science of the present day should determine that the Church shall not through them be exposed to the reproach to which Descartes thus laid it open—namely, of actually impeding scientific progress. They should in no wise allow their efforts after truth to be checked by the declaration of ecclesiastical authorities, seeing clearly now that the faithful Catholics who held true doctrine in the seventeenth century were the condemned and not the condemners. Mr. Murphy tells us as to evolution, that 'so direct, so precise, so circumstantial, is the Scriptural account of man's creation, that, if the evolution theory were true, the sacred writings, if they intended to deceive us, could not have chosen language better calculated to effect that end.' Might not the very same thing be said as to the Scripture account of the universality of the Deluge, the universal destruction outside the ark of men and animals, if the Deluge was *not* universal, and if multitudes not only of animals, but even of men, outside that ark, were, in fact, *not* destroyed? Yet an English Catholic Bishop [18] tells us we may hold that men as well as animals were not so destroyed.

Exegesis is not my study, I have no skill in, or knowledge of it; I only judge what to believe in this matter according to the light of science, and that light shows me that it was impossible for all animals to have been destroyed, and I judge similarly with respect to the general doctrine of evolution.

How much latitude has existed in the Church even in the early days of the triumphs which physical science has not ceased to enjoy for the last four centuries, is plain from the following judgments publicly emitted by the great Roman theologian Cajetan.[19] He was made a cardinal in 1517, and sent as legate to Germany in 1518. In 1519 he was made Bishop of Gaeta, and in 1523 was sent as legate to Hungary.

[18] The Hon. and Right Rev. Bishop Clifford.

[19] The present Pontiff, when requested by an Italian bishop to specify what commentators on St. Thomas he recommended, replied, Cardinal Cajetan and Franciscus Ferrariensis, Franciscus being the commentator on the philosophy, but Cajetan on the *theology* of St. Thomas!

In his great commentary on Holy Scripture [20] he teaches that the account of the creation of Eve is but a sort of parable intended to show the intimacy of the marriage tie; that the serpent described as speaking to Eve is only the symbol of an *internal* temptation; with other interpretations equally free. As to a belief in the literal truth of Eve's creation, he does not hesitate to call it ' *absurd*.' He never was compelled to retract his statements, still less was excommunicated in default of so doing.

We may now turn to consider the special question at issue between most biologists and a certain number of theologians. I mean the question of evolution.

As to the truth of the doctrine of evolution generally and in some form, it would be a waste of time and space at this day to argue at any length in its favour. Its truth is generally conceded, and may at any time suddenly become a matter of sensible experience. It is otherwise, of course, as regards the question concerning man's bodily origin, the mode of which must remain a matter of analogical inference; and, as Darwin himself has remarked, analogy is a misleading guide. Nevertheless, a high scientific probability may attach to a physical truth inaccessible to demonstration, as, for example, the probability that the side of the moon we can never see is not of a totally different nature and aspect from that side of it which we do see. I have already on several occasions tried to show that different considerations point in different directions as to the problem of man's bodily origin : (1) the similarity between the phenomena presented by the bodies of men and certain animals both in their adult condition and in their process of development, points to a similarity between their modes of origin; (2) the dissimilarity between their mental natures points to a dissimilarity between their modes of origin in so far as man's body may be inseparably connected with his mental nature. It is thus conceivable that God might or might not have miraculously created the human body, though analogy is strongly in favour of its natural evolution.

It has been urged by Darwin and others that God would have deceived us if He had made a body with all the physical signs of evolution but which had not been in fact evolved. This does not, however, appear to me to involve any moral difficulty, on the view that theologians have no more right to dictate what is to be our belief in this matter than to dictate what shall be our belief as to the revolution of the earth or as to the number of ages during which it has been the theatre of human activity. We are then in no way bound to arrive at a correct solution of the problem, nor is that solution of any practical importance to us. By the grace of God we are what we are, and we have the same lofty intellectual nature and the same responsibility, whether the matter of our material

---

[20] This work will be found in the British Museum library under the title : ' Vio (Thomas de) Cardinal : Old Testament, Pentateuch *Commentarii* . . . *in quinque Mosaicos libros*. 1539. Folio Press Mark 1008, e. 12 (1).'

frame came to us directly from the inorganic world or indirectly through the ministry of our lower fellow-creatures. The moral aspect of the question, however, would become quite changed if we were required to believe that *our eternal destiny* depended in part on our *not making a mistake* in this matter. In that case it seems clear that a good God, however much He might test our will by allowing certain difficulties to attend the evidences of religion, could never have miraculously created a number of corporeal characters all pointing to a conclusion to accept which would involve our damnation, and not a single character pointing towards the one only conclusion which would be absolutely necessary for our salvation. Must not such a belief involve a complete and unavoidable moral contradiction? This is a question which each man's conscience must answer. Let our beliefs in this matter be supposed free and unfettered as to their consequences, and then either origin of man's corporeal frame is conceivable; but let a belief in its miraculous creation be admitted as a condition upon which alone we can escape eternal torments, and then the conclusion seems to me irresistible, that a body directly and independently formed with characters so fatally misleading could never have been the creation of a God of truth and goodness, but rather of a malignant Father of lies!

A writer such as Mr. Murphy should carefully inform himself of the scientific as well as the ecclesiastical bearings of the question before he ventures to press upon our acceptance, as he does, a doctrine so inexpressibly shocking as that our eternal happiness depends upon our believing in the miraculous and sudden creation of the bodies of Adam and Eve. Nothing could well be more prejudicial to the cause which Mr. Murphy may be supposed to have at heart than the production of a widespread conviction that loyal Church-membership necessitates the acceptance of anything which at one and the same time revolts both our conscience and our scientific judgment.

No decree of Pope or Council can, however, be quoted as condemning evolution, and I venture to predict that it will be a long time before even any such authoritative condemnation can be cited against that doctrine as can be cited against the doctrine of the earth's diurnal and orbital motion. But the Rev. Mr. Murphy himself concedes that no judgment was passed that was indisputably *ex cathedra* even against Copernicanism. *A fortiori*, then, no authoritative judgment whatever has yet issued against evolution. As, however, no one can venture to affirm that more pressure may not be brought to bear against evolution than has yet been brought to bear against it, men who are both honest students of science and loyal children of the Church may be fairly expected by non-Catholics to state candidly the position they would be prepared to take up in the event of any such pressure.

A loyal Catholic must of course say that when any matter is clearly of faith, his conclusions must be wrong if they are opposed to it. But after all, and in every case, he has but his judgment to rely on as to the fact, or nature, of the supposed conflict. It is only through his own reason, informed by his senses, that he can possibly know that any decision whatever has been made (supposing it to have been made), and therefore he has always the choice whether to distrust the fact of the decision or the fact of physical science.

But though nothing can be quoted as at once certainly *ex cathedra* and at the same time opposed to evolution, yet pronouncements which some theologians deem infallible utterances seem to have been issued against such a minimising of the authority of ecclesiastical judges and congregations as is here contended for. This I should not be candid if I did not admit. It is true that the Pope, in his celebrated Munich brief, does bid men of science submit themselves to such authorities.

Certain utterances then may be cited in opposition to the views here advocated, and I shall be asked how I reconcile them with the 'Mirari vos,' the 'Quanta cura,' and the 'Syllabus.' I might reply to such a question in the language of many theologians who, when confronted with perplexing declarations of physical science, content themselves with replying that 'truth cannot contradict truth,' and that there must be therefore some satisfactory explanation of such apparent conflicts. I should shortly reply, however, in the words of the Jesuit Father Hill: 'the criterion of scientific and philosophical truth is not authority, but evidence.' I decline to attempt the task of furnishing an interpretation of legal ecclesiastical documents for which I have not the requisite technical knowledge, but I am quite sure that authority can be justified only by reason, and cannot, therefore, be justified if it opposes reason. The error of Galileo's condemnation, as I have said, is not likely to be repeated nowadays, but if *per impossibile* authority was ever to demand the affirmation that death first absolutely came into the world after Adam's sin, it would be simply impossible for us in the face of the many palæozoic fossils, to make such an affirmation. If supreme authority and intuitive truth could and did come into collision, then authority would simply stultify itself. For it is a recognised canon of logic, that if any authority denies any proposition supported by a preponderance of evidence, that authority loses claim to our submission in whatever degree the evidence for the proposition is greater than that for the authority itself. Nor has even supreme authority a right to protest against such a hypothetical proposition as that just made, since St. Paul himself gives us an example of the kind when he says: 'If Christ be not risen, then is our preaching vain, and your faith is also vain' (1 Cor. xv. 14). No one could be so unreasonable as to affirm that language may not be used respecting the Church which may be freely used respecting the Church's Lord and Master. So to affirm would at least indicate a tone of mind certainly unapostolic.

For my own part—in spite of my love of science, which is the deepest seated and most rooted feeling I possess, and though the study of biology has been the main occupation of my life, yet I have never made exaggerated claims in its name. Strongly impressed with the intrinsically relative insignificance of *all* physical questions when compared with those which relate to man's noblest aspirations and best future hopes, I have ever deemed it my highest privilege to be allowed to point out the essential harmony which exists between the truths of science and the dictates of religion.

It is not lightly, then, nor without a deep sense of responsibility that I give my testimony to what I believe to be a truth alike necessary for either cause.

I well know that many anxious inquirers amongst Catholics are seeking how best to fulfil their duties both to their science and to their faith. To such inquirers I venture to offer the considerations here put forward, which will, I trust, furnish a reply to Mr. Murphy, and at the same time help to guide the Catholic man of science as to his duty. His duty appears to me to be clear. He owes to God the faithful and industrious use of the talent entrusted to him, undeterred by the clamour of well-meaning but incompetent obstructives. As a truly loyal son of the Church he should be careful that she may never through him incur the reproach of hampering and impeding the course of science. Bearing in mind the wise warning of Cardinal Pitra and the ever-memorable words (before quoted) of Leo XIII., on the one hand, and the lesson taught by the history of the seventeenth century on the other, I conceive it to be the duty of the Catholic man of science, whether cleric or layman, calmly to pursue his scientific investigations, with the aid of such theories as may best help him on his way. He may also, I am persuaded, comfort himself with the assurance that the supreme rulers in the domain of theology will now view with favour and approval, rather than with jealousy and reprobation, the rapid development of that branch of knowledge which concerns itself with organic life, and with all that relates to the merely animal nature of man—the science of Biology.

The strange result, then, of the seventeenth century struggle—a result as happy as it was one impossible to foresee—has been the permanent enlargement of Catholic intellectual liberty in every department of science without exception, to a degree which not the most sanguine of our predecessors could have hoped for; and this result has only recently been made manifest by the defeated efforts of the extreme infallibilists of the era of the Vatican Council. The cause of evolution, then, in any subsequent struggle is gained before that struggle has begun, and we have to thank the once for all happily decided battle between theologians and astronomers for having made once for all superfluous any such subsequent battle between evolutionists and theologians.

St. George Mivart.

www.ingramcontent.com/pod-product-compliance
Lightning Source LLC
Chambersburg PA
CBHW020248090426
42735CB00010B/1862